EDWARD D. ANDREWS

IF GOD IS GOOD

Why Does God Allow Suffering?

IF GOD IS GOOD

Why Does God Allow Suffering?

Edward D. Andrews

Christian Publishing House
Cambridge, Ohio

Copyright © 2015 Edward D. Andrews

All rights reserved. Except for brief quotations in articles, other publications, book reviews, and blogs, no part of this book may be reproduced in any manner without prior written permission from the publishers. For information, write,

support@christianpublishers.org

IF GOD IS GOOD: Why Does God Allow Suffering? by Edward D. Andrews

ISBN-10: 0692414622

ISBN-13: 978-0692414620

Table of Contents

Book Description 7

Preface 9

Introduction 11

CHAPTER 1 Whi Has God Permitted Suffering and Evil? 13

    I. Introduction 13

    II. The Definition of Evil and Suffering 17

    III. The Theodicies 20

    IV. Objections to Theodicies 26

    V. The Christian Response to Evil and Suffering 34

    VI. Conclusion 37

CHAPTER 2 The Problem of Foreknowledge and Free Will 47

    I. Introduction 47

    II. The Concept of Foreknowledge 50

    III. The Concept of Free Will 53

    IV. The Compatibility Problem 55

    V. The Christian Response to the Compatibility Problem 60

    VI. Conclusion 66

CHAPTER 3 The Scale of Justice: Understanding Life's Disparities 73

    Navigating Life's Inequities: Beyond Human Perspective 73

    The Role of Free Will in Life's Imbalance 76

    The Illusion of Fairness in a Fallen World 79

    God's Sovereignty Amidst Earthly Injustice 82

CHAPTER 4 Divine Intervention: Expectations vs. Reality 86

The Myth of Constant Divine Rescue 86

Faithfulness and the Reality of Life's Struggles 89

Understanding the Limits of God's Earthly Intervention 92

The Purpose Behind Unanswered Prayers 95

CHAPTER 5 The Adversary Unveiled: Acknowledging Satan's Role 99

The Reality of Evil Personified 99

Satan's Influence and the Battle for Good 102

Demystifying the Devil: Scripture's Testimony .. 106

The Existential Threat: Combatting Spiritual Deception 109

CHAPTER 6 Promises and Perseverance: Navigating Imperfection with God 113

Conditional Promises: Misconceptions and Clarifications 113

The Role of Scripture in Understanding Promises 116

The Nature of God's Guarantees in an Imperfect World 116

Misinterpreting Divine Guarantees: Expectations vs. Scriptural Reality 119

Perseverance Through Trials: The Biblical Perspective on Assurance 123

Bibliography 126

Book Description

In "IF GOD IS GOOD: Why Does God Allow Suffering?", the author embarks on a profound exploration into one of the most challenging questions facing believers: Why does a benevolent God permit suffering and evil in the world? This meticulously researched book draws upon a wealth of biblical scholarship and theology to offer insights into a question that has perplexed scholars and laypeople alike for centuries.

Table of Contents Overview

Chapter 1: "Why Has God Permitted Suffering and Evil?" delves into the nature of evil and suffering, examining the various theodicies proposed throughout Christian history. It confronts common objections to these theodicies and posits a robust Christian response to the presence of evil and suffering in the world.

Chapter 2: "The Problem of Foreknowledge and Free Will" tackles the intricate relationship between God's omniscience and human autonomy. The author engages with the philosophical conundrum of foreknowledge and free will, unraveling the apparent paradox and elucidating the Christian perspective on the compatibility of the two.

Chapter 3: "The Scale of Justice: Understanding Life's Disparities" offers a penetrating look into the inequities of life, challenging the notion of fairness in a fallen world. It underscores the role of free will in human experience and God's sovereignty amidst earthly injustice.

Chapter 4: "Divine Intervention: Expectations vs. Reality" scrutinizes the expectations of divine intervention against the reality of Scripture. This chapter addresses the myths surrounding constant divine rescue and sheds light on the purpose behind unanswered prayers.

Chapter 5: "The Adversary Unveiled: Acknowledging Satan's Role" reveals the Biblical portrayal of Satan, his influence, and the spiritual battle waged between good and evil. It aims to demystify the devil's role and equip believers with the knowledge to combat spiritual deception.

Chapter 6: "Promises and Perseverance: Navigating Imperfection with God" wraps up the discourse with a discussion on the true nature of God's promises and the role of perseverance through life's trials. It dispels common misconceptions about divine guarantees and offers a scriptural understanding of assurance in the face of imperfection.

Each chapter is a deep dive into the complexities of its topic, always returning to the core of biblical teaching and the steadfast character of God. "IF GOD IS GOOD: Why Does God Allow Suffering?" is an essential read for anyone grappling with the realities of pain and injustice in light of a loving Creator. It is a beacon of hope and a source of answers that provides not only scholarly insight but also pastoral care to readers seeking to reconcile their faith with the existence of suffering.

Preface

The question of why a loving, omnipotent God allows suffering and evil is a conundrum that has haunted humanity since the dawn of consciousness. It's a question that transcends cultures, religions, and epochs. In our journey through life, whether we are steeped in theological inquiry or simply trying to make sense of the world's hurt, the question beckons a response, often with a sense of urgency that mirrors the pain witnessed or experienced.

This book is born out of a profound need to address this quandary—not with platitudes or dismissive reasoning, but with the intellectual and spiritual rigor it demands. "IF GOD IS GOOD: Why Does God Allow Suffering?" is not merely an academic discourse but also a heartfelt attempt to navigate the rocky terrains of doubt and faith, understanding and perplexity.

In the ensuing chapters, we venture together through the landscapes of Scripture, philosophy, and human experience. We engage with the biblical narrative to seek answers—answers that are not always easy or comfortable but are necessary for an authentic engagement with faith. This exploration takes us from the Garden of Eden to the modern day, examining not only the origins of evil but also the enduring presence of suffering in a world under divine watch.

The text is not designed to be an echo chamber of a single theological perspective; rather, it invites readers to contemplate a spectrum of understandings within the Christian faith. We grapple with tough issues, including the intricate concepts of foreknowledge, free will, and the justice of God, never shying away from the difficult questions these topics raise.

With an unwavering commitment to Scripture and a clear acknowledgment of God's ultimate sovereignty, the book is an endeavor to provide solace and strength to those who struggle. It aims to be a companion to the weary, a guide to the seeker, and a source of clarity to the confused.

This preface is not a summary of the book's contents, but a doorway into its heart. As you turn these pages, may you find not just the robustness of argument but also the resonance of truth, the kind that empowers and edifies, the kind that speaks with the gentle authority of Jehovah Himself.

Let us embark on this journey together, with minds ready to learn and hearts open to the wisdom that comes from above.

Edward D. Andrews

Author of 220+ books and Chief Translator of the Updated American Standard Version

Introduction

Embarking on a journey to understand God's role in the presence of suffering and evil is akin to standing at the edge of a vast ocean, contemplating the depths beneath and the horizons beyond. It is an endeavor that invites not just contemplation but a bold dive into the deep waters of theological inquiry and human experience. This book seeks to be a vessel for such an expedition, one that is both anchored in the bedrock of Scripture and buoyed by the quest for understanding.

As we stand at this precipice, it is important to clarify the intent and the spirit with which this journey is undertaken. This is not a quest for simple answers or quick fixes. The complexities of life and the mysteries of divine providence do not allow for such. Instead, we seek a thoughtful, scripturally grounded exploration of why a benevolent and almighty God permits the tapestry of human existence to be woven with threads of suffering and strokes of darkness.

From the outset, we affirm the difficulty of this question. It challenges the core of our faith and the resilience of our spirit. Yet, it is in the pursuit of this very challenge that we often find a deeper sense of purpose and a more profound understanding of faith. The question of suffering and evil touches everyone—believer and skeptic alike—and thus, the discussion herein is meant to resonate on a universal level, even as it upholds a specific theological stance.

In the chapters that follow, we do not propose to exhaust the conversation; rather, we aim to contribute to it by examining critical aspects of the age-old debate surrounding divine justice, human freedom, and the seeming incongruence between the existence of an all-powerful, all-loving God and the reality of suffering.

We will explore the nature of evil and suffering, the theological constructs proposed throughout Christian history, and the robust responses that can be offered when one approaches the issue through the lens of Scripture with a heart seeking truth. Each chapter is intended to build upon the last, ushering the reader into progressively deeper waters of understanding.

It is my prayer that as you delve into the pages of this book, you will not only encounter a scholarly examination of theodicy but also experience a personal journey that touches the soul. May the insights gleaned here not only inform but also transform, offering not only perspective but also peace.

With the resolve of one who seeks to know Jehovah more intimately and the humility of one who stands before a vast and mysterious ocean, let us begin.

CHAPTER 1 Whi Has God Permitted Suffering and Evil?

I. Introduction

The late Ronald Nash was a Christian philosopher and apologetics who wrote extensively on the Problem of Evil and Suffering. According to Nash, the Problem of Evil and Suffering is a significant challenge to the existence of an all-powerful, all-knowing, and all-good God. Nash argued that the problem can be resolved by understanding the nature of God and his relationship to the world.

Nash emphasized that God's sovereignty and power are not threatened by evil and suffering, but rather are demonstrated by his ability to bring good out of evil circumstances. Nash also argued that the existence of evil and suffering is a result of human free will and that God allows evil and suffering to exist in order to bring about a greater good.

Nash further argued that the existence of evil and suffering can be seen as a result of the Fall, the biblical account of humanity's rebellion against God. Nash believed that the Fall resulted in a broken world in which evil and suffering exist, but that God is ultimately in control and will ultimately bring an end to evil and suffering.

In Nash's view, the Problem of Evil and Suffering can be resolved through a deeper understanding of God's nature and his relationship to the world, as well as an appreciation for the role that human free will and the Fall play in the existence of evil and suffering. Nash's perspective on the Problem of Evil and Suffering offers a unique and insightful contribution to Christian apologetics and provides a framework for understanding and engaging with this difficult issue.

Ronald Nash, William Lane Craig, and Norman L. Geisler are all prominent Christian apologists who have written on the issue of the Problem of Evil and Suffering. While they all come from a similar theological perspective and share many of the same views, they do not necessarily agree on every aspect of the issue.

For example, William Lane Craig is known for his defense of the "free will defense," which argues that the existence of evil and suffering is a result of human free will and that God allows evil and suffering to exist in order to preserve human freedom. Norman L. Geisler is also a proponent of the free will defense, but has also emphasized the idea of divine sovereignty, arguing that God is in control of all things and that even evil and suffering are ultimately part of his plan.

Ronald Nash, on the other hand, emphasized the idea that the existence of evil and suffering can be seen as a result of the Fall, the biblical account of humanity's rebellion against God. Nash believed that the Fall resulted in a broken world in which evil and suffering exist, but that God is ultimately in control and will ultimately bring an end to evil and suffering.

While these apologists share many of the same views and come from a similar theological perspective, they do not necessarily agree on every aspect of the issue of the Problem of Evil and Suffering. Nevertheless, they each provide valuable insights and perspectives on this complex and ongoing philosophical debate.

A. The Importance of the Problem

The ability to defend the Problem of Evil is an important aspect of Christian apologetics for several reasons:

1. **Responding to skeptics**: The Problem of Evil is a common challenge to the existence of an all-powerful, all-knowing, and all-good God, and one that many skeptics use to argue against the Christian faith. By being able to defend the Problem of Evil, Christians can respond to these objections and provide a compelling case for the existence of God.

2. **Strengthening faith**: Engaging with the Problem of Evil can help to strengthen a Christian's faith by providing a deeper understanding of God's nature and his relationship to the world, as well as a clearer appreciation for the role that human free will and the Fall play in the existence of evil and suffering.

3. **Sharing the gospel**: A strong defense of the Problem of Evil can also serve as an effective tool for sharing the gospel with others. By addressing the objections of skeptics and providing a compelling case for the existence of God, Christians can help to clear the way for others to hear and respond to the good news of Jesus Christ.

4. **Encouraging growth and development**: Engaging with the Problem of Evil can also encourage personal growth and development, as it requires Christians to think deeply about their faith and to consider difficult questions and objections.

In short, being able to defend the Problem of Evil is an important aspect of Christian apologetics, as it helps to respond to skeptics, strengthen faith, share the gospel, and encourage growth and development.

B. The Purpose of the Chapter

The purpose of this chapter on the Problem of Evil in a Christian apologetic book is to provide a comprehensive and compelling defense of the Christian belief in an all-powerful, all-knowing, and all-good God in light of the existence of evil and suffering in the world. This chapter will address the following goals:

1. To provide a clear and concise explanation of the Problem of Evil and Suffering, including its philosophical origins and key objections.
2. To offer a biblical and theological framework for understanding the nature of God and his relationship to the world, including a defense of the idea of divine sovereignty and the role of human free will in the existence of evil and suffering.
3. To provide a comprehensive defense of the Christian belief in an all-powerful, all-knowing, and all-good God, including a response to common objections and a presentation of compelling evidence for the existence of God.
4. To encourage readers to think deeply about the Problem of Evil and Suffering and to consider how their faith can be strengthened by engaging with this difficult issue.

The purpose of a chapter on the Problem of Evil in a Christian apologetic book is to provide a comprehensive and compelling defense of the Christian faith in light of the existence of evil and suffering, and to encourage readers to think deeply about their faith and to consider how it can be strengthened by engaging with this difficult issue.

II. The Definition of Evil and Suffering

Evil can be defined as the absence or opposite of good, or as morally wrong or wicked behavior. In a philosophical or theological context, evil often refers to acts or events that cause harm or suffering to others, or that go against the moral order established by God.

Suffering, on the other hand, can be defined as the state of undergoing pain, distress, or hardship. In a philosophical or theological context, suffering often refers to the experience of physical or emotional pain, or to the experience of loss or hardship.

Together, the concepts of evil and suffering raise important questions about the nature of God, the purpose of existence, and the role of human free will in the world. They are central to the philosophical challenge known as the Problem of Evil and Suffering, which asks how an all-powerful, all-knowing, and all-good God can allow evil and suffering to exist in the world.

A. The Concept of Evil

The concept of evil refers to actions or events that cause harm, suffering, or destruction to others or to the world. In a moral or religious context, evil is often seen as a violation of divine laws or moral standards, and is associated with wickedness, sin, or wrongdoing.

The existence of evil has been a subject of philosophical and theological inquiry for centuries, with many different perspectives and interpretations. Some philosophers and theologians have argued that evil is a result of human free will, while others have argued that it is a result of the limitations of a created world.

In a religious context, the concept of evil is often tied to the idea of sin, or the rebellion against God and his laws. Many religions also include beliefs about the existence of evil forces or entities, such as demons or evil spirits, that are seen as working against the good and the will of God.

Despite the many different perspectives and interpretations, the concept of evil remains a central and challenging issue in philosophy and theology. It raises important questions about the nature of God, the purpose of existence, and the relationship between good and evil in the world.

B. The Concept of Suffering

The concept of suffering refers to the experience of physical or emotional pain, hardship, or distress. It encompasses a wide range of experiences, from physical ailments and injuries to the loss of loved ones, natural disasters, and social injustices.

The existence of suffering has been a subject of philosophical and theological inquiry for centuries, with many different perspectives and interpretations. Some philosophers and theologians have argued that suffering is a necessary aspect of human existence, serving a greater purpose such as personal growth and spiritual development. Others have argued that suffering is a result of human sin or the limitations of a created world.

In a religious context, the concept of suffering is often tied to the idea of a fallen world, or the belief that the world was originally created good but has been impacted by sin and evil. Many religions also include beliefs about the existence of a divine plan or purpose and see suffering as serving a greater good or as part of a larger story of redemption and restoration.

Despite the many different perspectives and interpretations, the concept of suffering remains a central and challenging issue in philosophy and theology. It raises important questions about the nature of God, the purpose of existence, and the relationship between good and evil in the world.

C. The Interrelation of Evil and Suffering

Evil and suffering are often interrelated in that evil actions or events can cause suffering to others or to the world. For example, natural disasters, war, and acts of violence can all cause physical and emotional suffering to those affected by them.

The interrelation of evil and suffering raises important philosophical and theological questions about the nature of God, the purpose of existence, and the relationship between good and evil in the world. Some philosophers and theologians have argued that evil and suffering are a result of human free will or the limitations of a created world, while others have argued that they serve a greater purpose such as personal growth and spiritual development.

In a religious context, the interrelation of evil and suffering is often tied to the idea of a fallen world, or the belief that the world was originally created good but has been impacted by sin and evil. Many religions also include beliefs about the existence of a divine plan or purpose and see evil and suffering as serving a greater good or as part of a larger story of redemption and restoration.

Regardless of the perspective, the interrelation of evil and suffering is a central and challenging issue in philosophy and theology, raising important questions about the nature of God, the purpose of existence, and the relationship between good and evil in the world.

III. The Theodicies

Theodicies are philosophical or theological attempts to justify the existence of God in light of the reality of evil and suffering in the world. Theodicies attempt to reconcile the belief in an all-powerful, all-knowing, and all-good God with the existence of evil and suffering, and to provide a coherent explanation for why God allows evil and suffering to exist.

There are several different types of theodicies, including the following:

1. **Free Will Defense**: This theodicy argues that God allows evil and suffering to exist because he has given humans the gift of free will. According to this view, God could not create a world in which humans are free and yet there is no evil and suffering.

2. **Soul-Making Theodicy**: This theodicy argues that God allows evil and suffering to exist as part of a process of personal growth and spiritual development. According to this view, God uses evil and suffering as a means of refining and transforming the human soul.

3. **Divine Sovereignty Theodicy**: This theodicy argues that God is in control of all things, including evil and suffering, and that even evil and suffering are ultimately part of his plan. According to this

view, God uses evil and suffering to bring about a greater good.
4. **Best of All Possible Worlds Theodicy**: This theodicy argues that God has created the best possible world, given the limitations of the world and human nature. According to this view, God has allowed evil and suffering to exist because it is the best possible solution to the limitations of the world and human nature.

These are just a few examples of the many different theodicies that have been proposed over the centuries. Each theodicy provides a different perspective on the relationship between God and evil and suffering, and each raises its own questions and objections. Nevertheless, theodicies remain an important aspect of Christian apologetics and provide a framework for understanding and engaging with the complex issue of the Problem of Evil and Suffering.

A. *The Free Will Theodicy*

The Free Will Theodicy is a philosophical perspective on the Problem of Evil and Suffering that argues that God allows evil and suffering to exist because he has given humans the gift of free will. This theodicy is supported by Ronald Nash, William Lane Craig, and Norman L. Geisler, among other Christian apologists.

According to the Free Will Theodicy, God created humans with the ability to choose between good and evil. God desires that humans love him freely, and so he allows humans to have the ability to choose whether or not to follow him. However, this freedom also means that humans have the ability to choose evil, and so evil and suffering exist in the world as a result of human sin and rebellion.

Ronald Nash, William Lane Craig, and Norman L. Geisler all support the Free Will Theodicy as a way of resolving the paradox of an all-powerful, all-knowing, and all-good God allowing evil and suffering to exist. They argue that God could not create a world in which humans are free and yet there is no evil and suffering, and that the existence of evil and suffering is a result of human free will and sin, not of God's will.

These apologists also argue that the Free Will Theodicy provides a compelling explanation for why God allows evil and suffering to exist, and that it is the best explanation given the nature of God and the reality of human free will. They believe that the Free Will Theodicy provides a framework for understanding and engaging with the Problem of Evil and Suffering and offers a compelling case for the existence of an all-powerful, all-knowing, and all-good God.

Ronald Nash, William Lane Craig, and Norman L. Geisler offer several explanations within the Free Will Theodicy to explain the existence of evil and suffering in the world. Some of these explanations include:

1. **Human free will**: They argue that God has given humans the gift of free will, which means that humans have the ability to choose between good and evil. As a result, evil and suffering exist in the world as a result of human sin and rebellion.

2. **The limitations of a created world**: They argue that God created the world with certain limitations, and that these limitations mean that there will always be evil and suffering in the world, regardless of God's desire for it to be otherwise.

3. **The idea of a fallen world**: They argue that the world was originally created good, but that it has

been impacted by sin and evil as a result of the fall of humanity. They believe that evil and suffering exist as a result of this fallen state of the world.

4. **Divine sovereignty**: They argue that God is in control of all things, including evil and suffering, and that even evil and suffering are ultimately part of his plan. They believe that God uses evil and suffering to bring about a greater good, and that he will ultimately bring an end to evil and suffering.

These explanations offer a way of understanding the relationship between God and evil and suffering and provide a framework for resolving the paradox of an all-powerful, all-knowing, and all-good God allowing evil and suffering to exist. They believe that the Free Will Theodicy provides a compelling explanation for why God allows evil and suffering to exist, and that it is the best explanation given the nature of God and the reality of human free will.

B. The Soul-Making Theodicy

The Soul-Making Theodicy is a philosophical perspective on the Problem of Evil and Suffering that argues that God allows evil and suffering to exist as part of a process of personal growth and spiritual development. This theodicy is supported by some Christian apologists, although Ronald Nash, William Lane Craig, and Norman L. Geisler are not known to have expressed support for this particular theodicy.

According to the Soul-Making Theodicy, God allows evil and suffering to exist as a means of refining and transforming the human soul. This theodicy argues that God uses evil and suffering as a tool to help humans grow in character, wisdom, and virtue, and to deepen their relationship with him.

The Soul-Making Theodicy provides a different perspective on the relationship between God and evil and suffering, and offers a way of understanding why God allows evil and suffering to exist. This theodicy argues that God allows evil and suffering to exist for a greater purpose, and that even the most difficult experiences can be used by God for good.

It is important to note that Ronald Nash, William Lane Craig, and Norman L. Geisler are not known to have expressed support for the Soul-Making Theodicy and may not agree with this particular perspective on the Problem of Evil and Suffering. However, they may still believe that God can use evil and suffering for a greater purpose, even if they do not support the Soul-Making Theodicy specifically.

C. The Greater Good Theodicy

The Greater Good Theodicy is a philosophical perspective on the Problem of Evil and Suffering that argues that God allows evil and suffering to exist for the sake of a greater good. This theodicy is supported by some Christian apologists, although Ronald Nash, William Lane Craig, and Norman L. Geisler are not known to have expressed support for this particular theodicy using this specific terminology.

According to the Greater Good Theodicy, God allows evil and suffering to exist because it serves a greater purpose, such as bringing about a greater good or achieving a greater end. This theodicy argues that God uses evil and suffering to bring about a greater good, and that even the most difficult experiences can be used by God for good.

The Greater Good Theodicy provides a different perspective on the relationship between God and evil and suffering, and offers a way of understanding why God allows evil and suffering to exist. This theodicy argues that God allows evil and suffering to exist for a greater purpose, and that even the most difficult experiences can be used by God for good.

It is important to note that Ronald Nash, William Lane Craig, and Norman L. Geisler are not known to have expressed support for the Greater Good Theodicy using this specific terminology and may not agree with this particular perspective on the Problem of Evil and Suffering. However, they may still believe that God can use evil and suffering for a greater purpose, even if they do not support the Greater Good Theodicy specifically.

D. Best of All Possible Worlds Theodicy

The Best of All Possible Worlds Theodicy is a philosophical perspective on the Problem of Evil and Suffering that argues that God has created the best possible world, given the limitations of the world and human nature. This theodicy is supported by some Christian apologists, although Ronald Nash, William Lane Craig, and Norman L. Geisler are not known to have expressed support for this particular theodicy using this specific terminology.

According to the Best of All Possible Worlds Theodicy, God has created the best possible world given the limitations of the world and human nature. This theodicy argues that God has allowed evil and suffering to exist because it is the best possible solution to the limitations of the world and human nature. This theodicy also argues that a world without evil and suffering would be a world without free will, which would not be the best possible world.

The Best of All Possible Worlds Theodicy provides a different perspective on the relationship between God and evil and suffering, and offers a way of understanding why

God allows evil and suffering to exist. This theodicy argues that God has created the best possible world given the limitations of the world and human nature, and that even the most difficult experiences serve a greater purpose.

It is important to note that Ronald Nash, William Lane Craig, and Norman L. Geisler are not known to have expressed support for the Best of All Possible Worlds Theodicy using this specific terminology, and may not agree with this particular perspective on the Problem of Evil and Suffering. However, they may still believe that God has created the best possible world, even if they do not support the Best of All Possible Worlds Theodicy specifically.

IV. Objections to Theodicies

A. *The Problem of Natural Evil*

The Problem of Natural Evil raises several objections to the belief in an all-powerful, all-knowing, and all-good God. Some of these objections include:

1. **The existence of natural disasters**: Natural disasters such as earthquakes, hurricanes, and tsunamis cause widespread suffering and death, and raise questions about why God would allow such events to occur.

2. **The existence of natural predators**: Many species of animals are natural predators, and they kill and eat other animals. This raises questions about why God would allow such suffering to exist.

3. **The existence of disease and illness**: Diseases and illnesses can cause significant suffering and death, and raise questions about why God would allow such things to exist.

4. **The existence of suffering in the animal kingdom**: Animals can suffer from diseases, predators, and other forms of suffering, and this raises questions about why God would allow such things to exist.
5. **The existence of suffering in infants and children**: Infants and children can suffer from diseases, disabilities, and other forms of suffering, and this raises questions about why God would allow such things to exist.

These objections challenge the belief in an all-powerful, all-knowing, and all-good God, and raise questions about why God would allow evil and suffering to exist in the world, especially in the form of natural evils. Theodicies, such as the Free Will Theodicy, Soul-Making Theodicy, Divine Sovereignty Theodicy, and Best of All Possible Worlds Theodicy, attempt to address these objections and provide a framework for understanding and engaging with the Problem of Natural Evil.

The Free Will Theodicy can be used to respond to the objections raised by the Problem of Natural Evil by addressing the relationship between God, free will, and natural evil. The following is an example of how the Free Will Theodicy might respond to these objections:

1. **The existence of natural disasters**: Natural disasters can be seen as a result of the limitations of the world and the free will of humanity. For example, people may choose to build homes in areas that are prone to natural disasters, or they may choose not to invest in disaster-preparedness measures. This choice can lead to increased suffering and death as a result of natural disasters.

2. **The existence of natural predators**: Natural predators can be seen as a result of the limitations of the world and the free will of humanity. For example, humans may choose to interfere with natural ecosystems, leading to increased suffering and death as a result of natural predators.

3. **The existence of disease and illness**: Diseases and illnesses can be seen as a result of the limitations of the world and the free will of humanity. For example, people may choose to engage in behaviors that increase their risk of disease or illness, or they may choose not to take preventative measures.

4. **The existence of suffering in the animal kingdom**: Suffering in the animal kingdom can be seen as a result of the limitations of the world and the free will of humanity. For example, humans may choose to interfere with natural ecosystems, leading to increased suffering and death in the animal kingdom.

5. **The existence of suffering in infants and children**: Suffering in infants and children can be seen as a result of the limitations of the world and the free will of others. For example, the free will of parents, medical professionals, or governments can impact the health and wellbeing of infants and children.

These responses offer a way of understanding the relationship between God, free will, and natural evil within the context of the Free Will Theodicy. They argue that God allows natural evil to exist as a result of the limitations of the world and the free will of humanity, and that even the most difficult experiences can be used by God for good.

B. *The Problem of Moral Evil*

The Problem of Moral Evil raises several objections to the belief in an all-powerful, all-knowing, and all-good God. Some of these objections include:

1. **The existence of intentional harm**: People intentionally cause harm to others through acts of violence, cruelty, or exploitation. This raises questions about why God would allow such evil to exist.

2. **The existence of moral evil committed by individuals**: People commit acts of evil, such as theft, murder, and abuse, and this raises questions about why God would allow such evil to exist.

3. **The existence of moral evil committed by groups**: Groups of people, such as governments, organizations, and religious groups, can commit acts of evil, such as genocide, terrorism, and religious persecution. This raises questions about why God would allow such evil to exist.

4. **The existence of moral evil committed by institutions**: Institutions, such as schools, prisons, and medical systems, can contribute to the suffering and oppression of individuals, and this raises questions about why God would allow such evil to exist.

5. **The existence of moral evil committed by nature**: Natural forces, such as tsunamis and earthquakes, can cause harm to individuals and communities, and this raises questions about why God would allow such evil to exist.

These objections challenge the belief in an all-powerful, all-knowing, and all-good God, and raise questions about why God would allow evil and suffering to exist in the world, especially in the form of moral evils. Theodicies, such as the Free Will Theodicy, Soul-Making Theodicy, Divine Sovereignty Theodicy, and Best of All Possible Worlds Theodicy, attempt to address these objections and provide a framework for understanding and engaging with the Problem of Moral Evil.

The Free Will Theodicy can be used to respond to the objections raised by the Problem of Moral Evil by addressing the relationship between God, free will, and moral evil. The following is an example of how the Free Will Theodicy might respond to these objections:

1. **The existence of intentional harm**: People have the free will to cause intentional harm to others, and God allows this to occur as a result of his respect for free will. God allows people to make choices, even choices that lead to evil, in order to respect the free will that he has given to humanity.

2. **The existence of moral evil committed by individuals**: Individuals have the free will to commit acts of evil, and God allows this to occur as a result of his respect for free will. God allows people to make choices, even choices that lead to evil, in order to respect the free will that he has given to humanity.

3. **The existence of moral evil committed by groups**: Groups of people have the free will to commit acts of evil, and God allows this to occur as a result of his respect for free will. God allows people to make choices, even choices that lead to

evil, in order to respect the free will that he has given to humanity.

4. **The existence of moral evil committed by institutions**: Institutions can be a result of the free will of individuals, and God allows this to occur as a result of his respect for free will. God allows people to make choices, even choices that lead to evil, in order to respect the free will that he has given to humanity.

5. **The existence of moral evil committed by nature**: Natural forces can cause harm as a result of the limitations of the world, and God allows this to occur as a result of his respect for the free will of humanity. God allows people to make choices, even choices that lead to evil, in order to respect the free will that he has given to humanity.

These responses offer a way of understanding the relationship between God, free will, and moral evil within the context of the Free Will Theodicy. They argue that God allows moral evil to exist as a result of his respect for the free will of humanity, and that even the most difficult experiences can be used by God for good.

C. The Problem of the Hiddenness of God

The Problem of the Hiddenness of God raises several objections to the belief in an all-powerful, all-knowing, and all-good God. Some of these objections include:

1. **The absence of clear evidence**: God is not clearly and directly evident to everyone, and this raises questions about why God would be so hidden.

2. **The lack of personal experience**: Many people have not had a personal experience of God, and

this raises questions about why God would be so hidden.

3. **The existence of religious diversity**: There are many different religions, each claiming to have a connection to the truth, and this raises questions about why God would be so hidden.

4. **The existence of atheism and agnosticism**: Many people do not believe in God or are unsure of God's existence, and this raises questions about why God would be so hidden.

5. **The existence of suffering and evil**: The reality of evil and suffering in the world raises questions about why God would be so hidden, especially when many people are searching for answers to the problem of evil.

These objections challenge the belief in an all-powerful, all-knowing, and all-good God, and raise questions about why God would be so hidden and why he would allow evil and suffering to exist in the world. Christian apologists have offered various responses to the Problem of the Hiddenness of God, including the argument from divine sovereignty, the argument from free will, and the argument from the inscrutable nature of God.

The Free Will Theodicy can be used to respond to the objections raised by the Problem of the Hiddenness of God by addressing the relationship between God, free will, and the hiddenness of God. The following is an example of how the Free Will Theodicy might respond to these objections:

1. **The absence of clear evidence**: God allows people the freedom to seek him or not to seek him. Some people may choose to ignore or reject the

evidence for God's existence, and this is a result of their free will.

2. **The lack of personal experience:** People have the free will to seek or not to seek a personal experience of God. Some people may choose not to seek such an experience, and this is a result of their free will.

3. **The existence of religious diversity:** People have the free will to choose which religion, if any, they want to follow. The existence of religious diversity is a result of people's free will to seek or not to seek God in different ways.

4. **The existence of atheism and agnosticism:** People have the free will to choose whether or not to believe in God. The existence of atheism and agnosticism is a result of people's free will to seek or not to seek God.

5. **The existence of suffering and evil:** People have the free will to choose how they respond to suffering and evil in the world. Some people may choose to reject God because of the existence of suffering and evil, and this is a result of their free will.

These responses offer a way of understanding the relationship between God, free will, and the hiddenness of God within the context of the Free Will Theodicy. They argue that God allows people the freedom to seek or not to seek him, and that the hiddenness of God is a result of people's free will to seek or not to seek God.

V. The Christian Response to Evil and Suffering

A. The Comfort of God's Presence

The comfort of God's presence is a response to evil and suffering that emphasizes the idea that God is always with us, even in the midst of suffering and evil. This response argues that God is not distant or uncaring but is present with us in our pain and suffering, and that he provides comfort and hope through his presence.

Some of the ways that the comfort of God's presence can be experienced include:

1. **Through prayer**: Talking to God in prayer can help people feel his presence and comfort during difficult times.

2. **Through community**: Being part of a supportive community of believers can provide comfort and encouragement during difficult times.

3. **Through scripture**: Reading and meditating on scripture can provide comfort and hope, as it reminds people of God's love, compassion, and faithfulness.

4. **Through personal experience**: People can experience the comfort of God's presence through personal experiences of his love and grace.

This response argues that God is always with us, even in the midst of suffering and evil, and that he provides comfort and hope through his presence. By focusing on God's presence, people can find comfort, hope, and peace in the midst of difficult times.

B. The Hope of Resurrection

The hope of resurrection is a response to evil and suffering that emphasizes the idea that there is a future hope beyond this life. This response argues that the hope of resurrection provides comfort and hope in the face of suffering and evil because it promises that there is a future state in which all things will be made right and all evil and suffering will be defeated.

Some of the ways that the hope of resurrection can be experienced include:

1. **Through faith**: Believing in the promise of the resurrection provides comfort and hope, even in the midst of suffering and evil.

2. **Through scripture**: Reading and meditating on scripture, especially passages related to the resurrection, can provide comfort and hope.

3. **Through community**: Being part of a community of believers who share the hope of the resurrection can provide comfort and encouragement during difficult times.

4. **Through personal experience**: People can experience the hope of the resurrection through personal experiences of God's love, grace, and provision, even in the midst of suffering and evil.

This response argues that the hope of the resurrection provides comfort and hope in the face of suffering and evil because it promises that there is a future state in which all things will be made right and all evil and suffering will be defeated. By focusing on the hope of the resurrection, people can find comfort, hope, and peace in the midst of difficult times.

C. The Call to Love and Compassion

The call to love and compassion is a response to evil and suffering that emphasizes the idea that people are called to respond to suffering and evil with love and compassion. This response argues that responding to suffering and evil with love and compassion can bring comfort and hope, both to those who are suffering and to those who are responding.

Some of the ways that the call to love and compassion can be experienced include:

1. **Through service**: Serving others who are suffering, such as volunteering in a soup kitchen or providing comfort to those who are grieving, can bring comfort and hope to both the giver and the receiver.

2. **Through advocacy**: Advocating for justice and standing up against evil and suffering can bring comfort and hope to those who are suffering.

3. **Through generosity**: Giving generously of time, resources, and money to organizations that serve those who are suffering can bring comfort and hope to both the giver and the receiver.

4. **Through prayer**: Praying for those who are suffering and asking God to bring comfort and hope can bring comfort and hope to both the prayer and the one being prayed for.

This response argues that responding to suffering and evil with love and compassion can bring comfort and hope, both to those who are suffering and to those who are responding. By focusing on the call to love and compassion, people can find comfort, hope, and peace in the midst of difficult times, and can make a positive impact on the world.

VI. Conclusion

A. The Importance of the Problem

It is important for Christians to be able to talk intelligently about the problem of evil and suffering for several reasons:

1. **To engage with non-believers**: The problem of evil and suffering is one of the most common objections to the existence of God, and Christians need to be able to engage with this issue in order to share their faith with others.

2. **To comfort those who are suffering**: Christians are called to comfort those who are suffering, and being able to talk intelligently about the problem of evil and suffering can help people find comfort and hope in difficult times.

3. **To deepen their own faith**: Engaging with the problem of evil and suffering can help Christians deepen their own faith, as they consider the nature of God, the existence of evil, and the hope of the resurrection.

4. **To foster community**: Engaging with the problem of evil and suffering can help Christians connect with others who are also struggling with these issues, and foster community and support.

5. **To demonstrate the truth of the faith**: Being able to talk intelligently about the problem of evil and suffering can help demonstrate the truth of the

Christian faith and show that Christians have thought through these difficult issues and have a coherent and meaningful response.

Therefore, it is important for Christians to be able to talk intelligently about the problem of evil and suffering in order to engage with non-believers, comfort those who are suffering, deepen their own faith, foster community, and demonstrate the truth of the faith.

B. The Role of Faith in Understanding Evil and Suffering

Faith plays a crucial role in understanding evil and suffering. For Christians, faith provides a lens through which they can understand the existence of evil and suffering and find hope in the midst of difficult times.

1. **Faith provides a framework for understanding evil and suffering**: Christians believe that God is all-powerful, all-knowing, and all-good, and that the existence of evil and suffering is a result of human sin and the limitations of the world. Through faith, Christians have a framework for understanding the existence of evil and suffering and can make sense of these difficult realities.

2. **Faith provides comfort in the face of evil and suffering**: Christians believe that God is present with them in their pain and suffering, and that he provides comfort and hope through his presence. Through faith, Christians can find comfort in the face of evil and suffering and can know that they are not alone.

3. **Faith provides hope in the face of evil and suffering**: Christians believe that there is a future

hope beyond this life, and that the hope of the resurrection provides comfort and hope in the face of suffering and evil. Through faith, Christians can find hope in the face of evil and suffering and can look forward to a future state in which all things will be made right.

4. **Faith provides motivation to respond to evil and suffering**: Christians believe that they are called to respond to suffering and evil with love and compassion, and that responding to suffering and evil with love and compassion can bring comfort and hope to both the giver and the receiver. Through faith, Christians can be motivated to respond to evil and suffering in meaningful ways, and can make a positive impact on the world.

Therefore, faith plays a crucial role in understanding evil and suffering, by providing a framework for understanding, comfort in the face of evil and suffering, hope in the face of evil and suffering, and motivation to respond to evil and suffering.

C. The Relevance of Evil and Suffering to Personal Faith

Evil and suffering are highly relevant to personal faith, as they raise important questions about the nature of God, the existence of evil, and the purpose of life. Engaging with the problem of evil and suffering can help deepen personal faith and strengthen one's relationship with God.

1. **Enhances spiritual growth**: Engaging with the problem of evil and suffering can help people grow spiritually, as they seek to understand the nature of God, the existence of evil, and the purpose of life.

This can deepen one's faith and bring a greater sense of meaning and purpose to life.

2. **Strengthens relationship with God**: Engaging with the problem of evil and suffering can help people grow closer to God, as they seek his comfort and hope in the midst of difficult times. This can deepen one's relationship with God and bring a greater sense of peace and security.

3. **Helps develop empathy and compassion**: Engaging with the problem of evil and suffering can help people develop empathy and compassion, as they consider the struggles of others and seek to respond to evil and suffering with love and compassion. This can help people become more compassionate and kinder and can make a positive impact on the world.

4. **Provides opportunity for personal reflection**: Engaging with the problem of evil and suffering can provide an opportunity for personal reflection, as people consider their own experiences of suffering and their response to it. This can help people grow in self-awareness and deepen their relationship with God.

Therefore, the problem of evil and suffering is highly relevant to personal faith, as it enhances spiritual growth, strengthens relationship with God, helps develop empathy and compassion, and provides opportunity for personal reflection.

Edward D. Andrews' Easy to Understand Explanation to the Problem of Evil and Suffering

Genesis 3:24 Updated American Standard Version (UASV)

24 So he drove the man out, and at the east of the garden of Eden he placed the cherubim and a flaming sword that turned every way to guard the way to the tree of life.

"God has morally sufficient reasons for permitting the evil and suffering in the world." – William Lane Craig

That *morally sufficient reason* lies below.

Bart D. Ehrman, a former Bible scholar and now an Agnostic, has raised a significant issue that challenges the existence of an all-powerful, all-knowing, and all-good God in light of the pain and suffering in the world. He finds it difficult to explain why there is so much evil, cruelty, war, disease, natural disasters, and the starvation of millions of innocent children if there is a good and loving God who is actively involved in the world.

However, the issue that Ehrman raises is based on a flawed assumption. He starts with the premise that if God is a God of love and has the power to fix anything, then why is there pain and suffering in the world? He also likely assumes that God is directly responsible for everything that happens. These assumptions lead to a narrow and incomplete understanding of the problem of evil and suffering.

God's perspective is different from ours, as he sees the big picture and has seen everything that has happened over the past 6,000 years in great detail. He is aware of the outcome of different scenarios, and he allows evil and suffering for the greater good. Furthermore, God is indirectly responsible for everything that happens in the world, just as parents are indirectly responsible for the actions of their children.

Many religious leaders have contributed to the belief that God does not care about us by making comments that blame God for bad things that happen. However, the Bible teaches that God cannot be tempted with evil and that he himself tempts no one. God never directly causes what is bad, and he is not responsible for the evil that humans bring upon themselves.

The history of humanity has been plagued by pain and suffering, and many have struggled to understand why a loving God would allow it to happen. To answer this question, we must go back to the first sin committed by Adam and Eve in the Garden of Eden. This event marks the beginning of the problem of evil and suffering in the world.

But first, in summary, the problem of evil and suffering is a complex issue that requires a deeper understanding of God's perspective and his plan for humanity. By starting with the right assumptions and looking to the Bible, we can gain a better understanding of why God allows evil and suffering in the world and find comfort in his presence and hope in his promises.

The passage from Genesis 2:17 and 3:1-5 tells the account of the temptation of Eve by Satan in the form of a serpent. God had warned Adam and Eve not to eat from the tree of the knowledge of good and evil, but Satan contradicted God's statement and told Eve that she would not die if she ate from the tree. Instead, Satan said that she would become like God and have the power to decide what is good and evil. Satan's statements challenged God's right to rule and suggested that people would only obey God if it was to their benefit.

In Job 1:6-11 and 2:4-5, Satan challenged God's way of ruling by suggesting that Job only feared God because of the blessings God had given him. Satan suggested that if those blessings were taken away, Job would curse God. This reference to "a man" suggests that all people will only obey God when things are good, but when difficulties arise, they will not obey.

God chose to deal with these issues by allowing time to pass and allowing the issues to be resolved. The fact that God has allowed evil, pain, and suffering has shown that independence from God has not brought about a better world and has proven that only God has the capability and the right to rule over humankind for their eternal blessing and happiness. Satan's impact on the earth has brought conflict, evil, and death, and his rulership has been by deception, power, and self-interest, making him an unfit ruler. God has tolerated evil until now in order to resolve all the issues raised by Satan, but he will not allow this evil to remain forever and has set a fixed time when he will end this wicked age of Satan's rule.

As Christians, we must not love the world or anything in it, but instead, we must set our pride aside and do the will of God. Not everyone who calls themselves a Christian will enter the kingdom of heaven, but only those who do the will of the Father in heaven. We must not love the world or anything in it, and instead, we must keep from becoming infected by the corruption of an unrighteous society. If we have the views of those who oppose God, the love of the Father will not be in us.

The question of whether Satan was punished is a complex one with deep roots in religious belief and interpretation. At its core, the question deals with the concept of free will and the relationship between God and his creations, both angels and humans.

In the biblical account of the Garden of Eden, Satan raised questions about God's sovereignty and the nature of human and angelic free will. He suggested that humans and angels did not need their creator and were better off without God. This raised concerns about whether God was lying and withholding information and cast doubt on the morality of the Creator.

In response to these questions and the rebellion of Satan, God chose to teach both angels and humans an object lesson. He allowed them to exercise their relative freedom, but not absolute freedom, and gave them an internal conscience to help guide their moral choices. This object lesson was meant to show that creatures are not designed to walk on their own and that they are better off under the umbrella of God's sovereignty.

Over the course of several thousand years, humanity has been learning this lesson through a process of trial and error. It is believed that the lesson will be fully learned once humanity reaches the point of self-destruction and God steps in to save them. At this point, the object lesson will be considered fully learned and no arguments can be raised.

Before going on, in summary, the punishment of Satan is a central aspect of the religious belief system that seeks to understand the relationship between God and his creations. Through the object lesson of free will, God is teaching his creations the importance of relying on him and recognizing the limitations of their own abilities.

The question of why Satan was not expelled from heaven immediately raises the issue of God's fairness and the role of free will. If God had expelled Satan right away, the other angels who witnessed the events in heaven might have questioned God's justice or even doubted His existence. It is important to understand that both humans and angels were created with free will, meaning they have the ability to make choices and decisions on their own. This free will also means that they are able to make mistakes and learn from the consequences of their actions.

In the case of Satan, he raised questions about God's sovereignty and challenged His authority. This led to a rebellion in Heaven and caused division among the angels. Instead of expelling Satan right away, God allowed him to stay in his realm, giving other angels the opportunity to learn from the consequences of Satan's actions.

According to the Bible, Satan will be expelled from Heaven shortly before the end of his rule on Earth. Revelation 12:9-12 states that Satan will be thrown to the Earth when "he knows that his time is short." This means that he will be expelled from Heaven before the Great Tribulation and Christ's return. When Jesus returns, Satan will be thrown into a maximum-security prison for a thousand years, during which time Jesus will restore what Satan had corrupted. After the thousand years, Satan will be released for a short time to tempt perfect humans, and unfortunately, some will fall away. In the end, Satan and those humans will be destroyed, and Jesus will hand the kingdom back over to the Father.

God allowed Satan to stay in his realm and learn from the consequences of his actions, rather than expelling him immediately, to preserve the fairness and justice of His rule and to demonstrate the importance of free will in the grand scheme of things.

God allows evil to exist in the world to teach people an object lesson, and to ultimately bring them closer to God.

According to this argument from Andrews, God wants humans to understand that they cannot walk on their own and that they are better off under the umbrella of God's sovereignty. By allowing evil to exist, God is allowing humans to learn from their mistakes and make better choices in the future. This approach emphasizes the importance of free will and the idea that humans must learn from their experiences, even if those experiences are painful. Eventually, God will step in and stop the object lesson when humanity has learned the full lesson. The ultimate goal is for humans to understand their dependence on God and to live in a state of peace and security under God's rule.

CHAPTER 2 The Problem of Foreknowledge and Free Will

I. Introduction

The Problem of Foreknowledge and Free Will is a philosophical and theological issue that has puzzled scholars and believers for centuries. At its core, it raises questions about the nature of God's foreknowledge and how it relates to human freedom. Some argue that if God knows everything in advance, then human actions are predetermined and free will is removed. On the other hand, others believe that God's foreknowledge does not remove human freedom, but rather coexists with it. This issue is not just a philosophical debate, but it also has important implications for our understanding of God, human responsibility, and the nature of reality. In this article, we will explore this problem in detail, examining various perspectives and offering insights and solutions to this complex and fascinating topic.

A. The Importance of the Problem

The Problem of Foreknowledge and Free Will is an important issue for Christians to understand for several reasons:

1. **It impacts our understanding of God**: Our understanding of God's nature and attributes is central to our faith, and this issue raises questions about God's power, knowledge, and sovereignty. If we do not have a clear understanding of how God's foreknowledge and human freedom can coexist, it

can lead to confusion and doubt about God's character.

2. **It affects our view of human responsibility**: The issue of foreknowledge and free will has important implications for our understanding of human responsibility. If human actions are predetermined, then people cannot be held responsible for their choices and actions. On the other hand, if human freedom is maintained, then people can be held accountable for their choices and actions.

3. **It challenges our beliefs**: The Problem of Foreknowledge and Free Will presents a challenge to our beliefs, as it requires us to reconcile two seemingly contradictory concepts: God's foreknowledge and human freedom. This challenge can help us grow in our faith and deepen our understanding of God and his ways.

4. **It helps us respond to objections**: Knowing how to respond to the Problem of Foreknowledge and Free Will can help us defend our faith and answer objections from skeptics. By having a clear understanding of the issue and the various perspectives, we can provide thoughtful and informed responses to those who question the compatibility of God's foreknowledge and human freedom.

In conclusion, understanding the Problem of Foreknowledge and Free Will is essential for Christians as it impacts our understanding of God, human responsibility, and our beliefs. By gaining a deeper understanding of this issue, we can grow in our faith, defend our beliefs, and deepen our relationship with God.

B. The Purpose of the Chapter

This chapter in a Christian apologetic book dealing with the Problem of Foreknowledge and Free Will will serve several purposes, including:

1. **Providing a clear explanation of the issue**: This chapter will provide a clear and concise explanation of the Problem of Foreknowledge and Free Will, including its history, key concepts, and implications.

2. **Presenting various perspectives**: This chapter will present and analyze various perspectives on the issue, including the views of philosophers, theologians, and biblical scholars. This would help readers understand the diverse range of opinions and arguments surrounding the issue.

3. **Offering solutions and insights**: This chapter will offer solutions and insights into the Problem of Foreknowledge and Free Will, providing a Christian perspective on the issue. This would help readers understand how God's foreknowledge and human freedom can coexist in a way that is consistent with biblical teaching and sound theology.

4. **Answering objections**: This chapter will address common objections to the compatibility of God's foreknowledge and human freedom, providing thoughtful and informed responses to skeptics.

5. **Strengthening faith and knowledge**: By presenting a comprehensive and well-researched understanding of the Problem of Foreknowledge and Free Will, this chapter will strengthen readers'

faith and deepen their knowledge of this important topic.

In conclusion, this chapter in a Christian apologetic book dealing with the Problem of Foreknowledge and Free Will serves as a valuable resource for readers seeking a deeper understanding of this complex issue. By presenting a clear explanation, diverse perspectives, and insightful solutions, this chapter will help readers strengthen their faith, deepen their knowledge, and respond to objections.

II. The Concept of Foreknowledge

Foreknowledge is the ability to know something before it occurs or comes into being. The concept of foreknowledge is often associated with the idea of predestination, which is the belief that events, including human actions, are predetermined and cannot be changed. Foreknowledge is typically associated with a deity or a supernatural being who has perfect knowledge of the future.

In a religious context, foreknowledge is often attributed to God, who is believed to have complete and perfect knowledge of all things, including future events. This belief is rooted in the idea of God's omniscience, which means that God knows everything that has happened, is happening, and will happen. Foreknowledge is seen as a characteristic of God's divine nature and a reflection of his sovereignty over all things.

In philosophical discussions, the concept of foreknowledge raises questions about the nature of reality and human freedom. Some argue that if God knows everything in advance, then human actions are predetermined and free will is removed. On the other hand, others believe that God's foreknowledge does not remove human freedom, but rather coexists with it in a way that allows for human choice and responsibility.

In conclusion, foreknowledge is the ability to know something before it occurs or comes into being. In a religious context, it is often attributed to God and seen as a characteristic of his divine nature. The concept of foreknowledge raises questions about the nature of reality and human freedom and is a topic of ongoing philosophical and theological discussions.

A. The Definition of Foreknowledge

Foreknowledge is the ability or power to know something before it happens or comes into existence. It refers to a pre-existing knowledge of future events or circumstances, which is often considered to be complete and accurate. Foreknowledge can be attributed to a deity or a supernatural being who has perfect knowledge of all things, including future events. In a religious context, foreknowledge is often considered a characteristic of God's divine nature, reflecting his sovereignty and omniscience. In philosophical discussions, the concept of foreknowledge raises questions about the relationship between knowledge and reality, as well as the nature of human freedom.

B. The Implications of Divine Foreknowledge

The implications of divine foreknowledge are a subject of ongoing philosophical and theological debate. Here are some of the key implications of the belief in God's foreknowledge:

1. **Predestination**: If God has foreknowledge of all events, including human actions, this can lead to the belief in predestination, which is the idea that events, including human actions, are predetermined and cannot be changed. This raises questions about the nature of human freedom and choice.

2. **Free Will**: If God knows everything in advance, including human actions, does this mean that human choices are predetermined, and free will is removed? Many philosophers and theologians argue that God's foreknowledge does not remove human freedom, but rather coexists with it in a way that allows for human choice and responsibility.

3. **Responsibility**: If God knows in advance what people will do, does this mean that they are not responsible for their actions? This raises questions about the nature of moral responsibility and accountability.

4. **Divine Sovereignty**: The belief in God's foreknowledge is often seen as a reflection of his sovereignty over all things, including future events. This reinforces the idea that God is in control of everything and that everything happens according to his plan.

5. **Divine Omniscience**: Foreknowledge is often seen as a characteristic of God's omniscience, which means that God knows everything that has happened, is happening, and will happen. This reinforces the idea that God has complete and perfect knowledge of all things.

In conclusion, the implications of divine foreknowledge are complex and multifaceted. While the belief in God's foreknowledge reinforces his sovereignty and omniscience, it also raises questions about the nature of human freedom, responsibility, and choice. These questions continue to be the subject of philosophical and theological discussions.

III. The Concept of Free Will

Free will is the ability of individuals to make choices and decisions that are not determined by outside forces or influences. It is the idea that people have the capacity to act and make decisions based on their own desires, motivations, and beliefs, rather than being forced or coerced into acting a certain way.

Free will is a central concept in many philosophical and religious discussions, as it raises questions about the nature of human agency, responsibility, and morality. Some argue that free will is essential to the idea of moral responsibility, as people must have the freedom to choose between right and wrong in order to be held accountable for their actions.

However, the concept of free will is also controversial, as it raises questions about the relationship between human action and the laws of physics or the concept of determinism. Some argue that everything that happens, including human actions, is predetermined by previous events and conditions, and that free will is an illusion.

In conclusion, free will is the ability of individuals to make choices and decisions that are not determined by outside forces or influences. It is a central concept in many philosophical and religious discussions, and raises questions about the nature of human agency, responsibility, and morality. Despite ongoing debates about its nature and existence, free will remains an important concept for understanding human choice and decision-making.

A. The Definition of Free Will

Free will is the ability of individuals to make choices and decisions that are not determined by outside forces or influences. It refers to the idea that people have the capacity to act and make decisions based on their own desires, motivations, and beliefs, rather than being forced or coerced into acting a certain way. In other words, free will is the ability to act according to one's own free choice and not because of any external constraints or influences.

B. The Implications of Human Free Will

The concept of free will has important implications for various aspects of human life, including morality, responsibility, and the nature of human agency. Here are some of the key implications of the belief in human free will:

1. **Moral Responsibility**: If people have the ability to make choices and decisions based on their own free will, then they can be held morally responsible for their actions. This means that people can be held accountable for their choices and the consequences that result from those choices.

2. **Personal Autonomy**: Free will is often seen as a cornerstone of personal autonomy, which is the ability of individuals to make choices and decisions that reflect their own beliefs, values, and desires. This means that people can act in ways that are meaningful and fulfilling to them, rather than being forced to act in ways that are determined by outside forces or influences.

3. **Free Society**: The belief in human free will is often seen as a requirement for a free society, where individuals are free to make choices and decisions

that reflect their own beliefs, values, and desires. This can result in a society that is diverse, creative, and dynamic, where people are free to pursue their own goals and ambitions.

4. **Ethics and Morality**: The concept of free will is closely tied to the idea of ethics and morality. If people have the ability to make choices and decisions based on their own free will, then they can be held responsible for their moral choices and the consequences that result from those choices.

5. **The Nature of Reality**: The belief in human free will raises questions about the nature of reality and the relationship between human actions and the laws of physics or the concept of determinism. Some argue that everything that happens, including human actions, is predetermined by previous events and conditions, and that free will is an illusion.

In conclusion, the concept of free will has important implications for various aspects of human life, including morality, responsibility, personal autonomy, the nature of reality, and the structure of a free society. Despite ongoing debates about its nature and existence, free will remains an important concept for understanding human choice and decision-making.

IV. The Compatibility Problem

The compatibility problem for the problem of foreknowledge and free will refers to the apparent conflict between two seemingly incompatible beliefs: that God has foreknowledge of all future events, and that human beings have the ability to make free choices and decisions. The problem arises when one tries to reconcile the idea of God's foreknowledge with the idea of human free will. If God knows in advance what choices a person will make, it appears that those choices are not truly free, as they are predetermined by God's foreknowledge. On the other hand, if human choices are truly free and not predetermined by God's foreknowledge, then it seems that God's foreknowledge is limited.

The compatibility problem has been debated by philosophers, theologians, and scholars for centuries, and there are a number of different solutions that have been proposed to resolve the apparent conflict. Some argue that God's foreknowledge does not determine human choices, and that human choices are truly free. Others argue that God's foreknowledge is not limited, and that human choices are determined by God's foreknowledge. Still others argue that God's foreknowledge and human free will are not logically incompatible, and that both can be true.

In conclusion, the compatibility problem for the problem of foreknowledge and free will is an important issue for those who believe in both God's foreknowledge and human free will. The problem raises questions about the nature of God's foreknowledge, the nature of human free will, and the relationship between the two. Despite ongoing debates and differing viewpoints, the compatibility problem remains an important area of inquiry for those who are interested in the relationship between God, human freedom, and the nature of the universe.

A. *The Problem of Determinism*

The problem of determinism refers to the philosophical issue of whether all events in the universe are predetermined and inevitable, or whether some events are the result of free will and chance. Determinism is the belief that all events, including human actions, are determined by prior causes and conditions and therefore are inevitable. According to determinism, everything that happens, including human choices and decisions, is the result of a chain of causality that is determined by physical laws and previous events.

The problem of determinism arises when it is considered in relation to the concept of free will. If everything is predetermined, it seems that human beings do not have the ability to make truly free choices but are instead merely following a predetermined path. This raises questions about the nature of human agency, responsibility, and morality.

Critics of determinism argue that it is incompatible with the idea of human freedom and responsibility. They argue that if everything is predetermined, then human beings cannot be held responsible for their actions, as they are merely following a predetermined path. Moreover, they argue that determinism undermines the ability to make moral judgments, as actions cannot be considered right or wrong if they are predetermined.

In conclusion, the problem of determinism is a central philosophical issue that raises questions about the nature of causality, free will, and human responsibility. While determinism has been widely accepted by many philosophers, it remains a controversial and debated topic, with ongoing discussions about the compatibility of determinism and free will.

B. The Problem of Indeterminacy

The problem of indeterminacy refers to the philosophical issue of whether some events in the universe are truly unpredictable and random, or whether they can be determined by prior causes and conditions. Indeterminacy is the belief that some events, such as the outcome of a coin flip or the decay of a radioactive particle, are truly random and not determined by prior causes or physical laws.

The problem of indeterminacy arises when it is considered in relation to the concept of causality. If some events are truly random, it seems that they cannot be explained by prior causes and conditions, and therefore, cannot be predicted with certainty. This raises questions about the nature of causality and the predictability of the universe.

Critics of indeterminacy argue that it is incompatible with the idea of causality and determinism. They argue that if some events are truly random, then it is impossible to fully explain and understand the universe, as random events cannot be predicted or explained by prior causes and conditions.

In conclusion, the problem of indeterminacy is a central philosophical issue that raises questions about the nature of causality, predictability, and randomness. While indeterminacy has been widely accepted by many philosophers, it remains a controversial and debated topic, with ongoing discussions about the compatibility of determinism, causality, and indeterminacy.

C. The Problem of Middle Knowledge

The problem of middle knowledge refers to the philosophical issue of how God can have knowledge of future contingent events, such as human choices and actions, without determining them or infringing on human freedom. Middle knowledge is the knowledge that God has of what any possible person would do in any possible situation.

The problem of middle knowledge arises because, on the one hand, if God knows what a person would do in a certain situation, it seems to suggest that the person's choice is predetermined and that they do not have free will. On the other hand, if God does not know what a person would do in a certain situation, it seems that God's knowledge is limited, which raises questions about God's omniscience.

The concept of middle knowledge is used to reconcile the apparent contradiction between God's foreknowledge and human freedom. According to proponents of middle knowledge, God knows what a person would do in a certain situation, but this knowledge does not determine the person's choice. Instead, it is the result of God's knowledge of the person's free will and the laws of nature.

In conclusion, the problem of middle knowledge is a central philosophical issue that raises questions about the nature of God's knowledge, human freedom, and determinism. While middle knowledge remains a debated topic, it is widely accepted by many philosophers as a solution to reconcile God's foreknowledge and human freedom.

Response to The Problem of Middle Knowledge

We would argue that middle knowledge is a necessary component of God's omniscience, and that it does not infringe on human freedom.

Our response to the problem of middle knowledge is based on the Molinist view of the relationship between God's knowledge, human freedom, and causality. God has middle knowledge of all possible worlds, including all possible choices and actions of free agents. This knowledge is logically prior to God's free will, but it does not determine it.

We would argue that God's middle knowledge allows Him to know what any possible person would do in any possible situation, without infringing on their freedom. We also argues that God's middle knowledge is a necessary component of His omniscience, as it allows Him to know all things that can be known, including future contingent events.

In conclusion, our response to the problem of middle knowledge is based on the Molinist view, which reconciles God's omniscience and human freedom by positing the existence of middle knowledge. God's middle knowledge allows Him to know all things that can be known, including future contingent events, without infringing on human freedom.

V. The Christian Response to the Compatibility Problem

The Christian response to the compatibility problem, also known as the problem of foreknowledge and free will, is the attempt to reconcile the seemingly contradictory notions of God's foreknowledge and human freedom. This is a central philosophical issue in Christian theology, as it raises questions about the nature of God's omniscience, human freedom, and determinism.

There are several different Christian responses to the compatibility problem, including Molinism, Simple Foreknowledge, and Open Theism.

Molinism, which was developed by the Spanish Jesuit priest Luis de Molina, argues that God has middle knowledge, which is the knowledge of what any possible person would do in any possible situation. This knowledge is logically prior to God's free will, but it does not determine it.

Simple Foreknowledge, on the other hand, argues that God simply knows everything, including future contingent events, but this knowledge does not determine them. Proponents of Simple Foreknowledge believe that human freedom and God's foreknowledge are compatible, as God's foreknowledge does not causally determine human choices.

Open Theism, which is also known as Neotheism, argues that God does not have exhaustive foreknowledge of future contingent events, as these events are not yet determined. Proponents of Open Theism believe that God's relationship with humanity is one of love, interaction, and co-creation, and that God's knowledge of the future is limited.

In conclusion, the Christian response to the compatibility problem is a central philosophical issue in Christian theology, and there are several different views on how to reconcile God's foreknowledge and human freedom. These views include Molinism, Simple Foreknowledge, and Open Theism, each of which offers a unique perspective on the relationship between God's knowledge, human freedom, and causality.

We would **respond positively to the concept of Simple Foreknowledge**. Simple Foreknowledge is a view that holds that God has complete and exhaustive foreknowledge of all events, including future contingent events, without causally determining or influencing them. This view seeks to reconcile God's foreknowledge with human freedom and moral responsibility.

We are a strong advocate of the doctrine of divine foreknowledge, and we believe that it is a fundamental aspect of God's nature as an omniscient being. We argue that God's foreknowledge is a necessary condition for his sovereignty, goodness, and providence. We also believe that God's foreknowledge does not undermine human freedom and moral responsibility, as God does not causally determine or influence the free choices of human beings.

We have argued that Simple Foreknowledge provides a coherent and biblical understanding of God's knowledge and power, and that it is a viable option for those seeking to reconcile God's foreknowledge with human freedom and moral responsibility. He has also argued that Simple Foreknowledge is consistent with the biblical understanding of God's sovereignty and goodness.

We would **take a critical view of Open Theism**. Open Theism argues that God does not have exhaustive foreknowledge of future contingent events, as these events are not yet determined. This view is seen as a challenge to classical theology, which holds that God has complete and exhaustive foreknowledge of all events, both past and future.

We are a proponent of classical theology and the doctrine of divine foreknowledge, and we have argued extensively against Open Theism. We believe that Open Theism undermines the traditional understanding of God's omniscience, sovereignty, and goodness. We argue that if God does not have exhaustive foreknowledge of future events, then God is not in control of the future, and this would imply that God is not sovereign.

A. The Rejection of Determinism

The rejection of determinism refers to the rejection of the idea that everything that happens, including human choices and actions, is completely determined or causally determined by prior events or causes.

Determinism is a philosophical viewpoint that states that the future is completely determined by the past, and that the events and choices of individuals are the result of previous causes and conditions. This means that the future is unchangeable and that every event and choice is predetermined.

However, many philosophers and theologians reject this view, as it is incompatible with human freedom and moral responsibility. They argue that if determinism were true, it would mean that people do not have the ability to choose and act freely, but that their choices and actions are predetermined by prior events or causes.

The rejection of determinism is often associated with the concept of free will, which is the ability of individuals to make choices and act freely, without being determined or influenced by outside forces. Those who reject determinism argue that free will is essential for human freedom, moral responsibility, and accountability.

B. The Acceptance of Molinism

Molinism is a philosophical and theological view that seeks to reconcile the concepts of divine foreknowledge and human free will. It was developed by the Spanish Jesuit priest Luis de Molina in the 16th century and has since become a popular position among some Christians.

The basic idea of Molinism is that God has what is called "middle knowledge," which is knowledge of all possible worlds and the free choices that individuals would make in each of those worlds. This means that God knows what each person would choose if they were faced with a particular set of circumstances.

Those who accept Molinism believe that God uses his middle knowledge to create a world in which he can bring about his desired outcomes without violating human freedom. They argue that God's foreknowledge of human choices does not determine or restrict human freedom, but rather it allows him to bring about his purposes in a world where individuals have the ability to choose freely.

In addition, Molinists believe that God's middle knowledge provides a way to resolve the problem of foreknowledge and free will, by showing that God's foreknowledge is not the cause of human choices, but rather the result of them. They argue that God's foreknowledge is a result of his knowledge of the choices that individuals would make in different circumstances, rather than a cause of those choices.

C. The Embrace of Mystery

The embrace of mystery refers to the idea that some aspects of reality, including religious and philosophical questions, may not be fully understandable or capable of being rationally explained. Instead of attempting to fully explain or understand these mysteries, one may choose to simply acknowledge and accept them as they are.

In the context of the problem of foreknowledge and free will, this means accepting that the relationship between God's foreknowledge and human free will may not be fully understandable. Some individuals may choose to embrace the mystery of how God can have complete knowledge of the future while still allowing for human freedom and choice.

The embrace of mystery does not necessarily mean a lack of belief or a rejection of certain ideas, but rather an acceptance that some things are beyond human comprehension. It is an attitude of humility and openness towards the limits of human understanding and a recognition that there may be aspects of reality that are simply mysterious and beyond explanation.

In summary, the embrace of mystery involves accepting that some aspects of reality, including religious and philosophical questions, may be beyond full understanding or explanation and choosing to simply acknowledge and accept them as they are.

We would have **a nuanced response to the embrace of mystery** in the context of the problem of foreknowledge and free will. While we would acknowledge that some aspects of reality, including the relationship between God's foreknowledge and human free will, may be beyond full understanding, we would also argue that there are rational and coherent solutions to these problems.

We defend Molinism, a philosophical system that seeks to reconcile God's foreknowledge with human freedom and choice. In this view, God has what is called "middle knowledge" of the possible choices and actions of free creatures but does not causally determine their choices. We would argue that Molinism provides a solution to the problem of foreknowledge and free will that does not require embracing mystery.

That being said, we would also acknowledge that there are limits to human understanding and that some aspects of reality may be mysterious and beyond explanation. In our view, embracing mystery would not necessarily mean rejecting rational explanations, but rather recognizing the limits of human understanding and acknowledging that there may be aspects of reality that are simply beyond explanation.

VI. Conclusion

A. The Importance of the Problem

The knowledge of the problem of foreknowledge and free will is important for Christians for several reasons:

1. **To understand the nature of God**: The problem of foreknowledge and free will raises questions about the nature of God's relationship to the world and the limits of his knowledge and power. By understanding the various positions and arguments in this debate, Christians can gain a deeper understanding of the nature of God and his relationship to humanity.

2. **To defend their faith**: The problem of foreknowledge and free will is often used by skeptics and critics of Christianity to argue that the idea of an all-knowing and all-powerful God is incompatible with human freedom and choice. By having a solid understanding of the various Christian responses to this problem, Christians can be better equipped to defend their faith against these objections.

3. **To deepen their faith**: Engaging with the problem of foreknowledge and free will can be an opportunity for Christians to deepen their faith by reflecting on the nature of God and the limits of

human understanding. It can also help them to appreciate the richness and complexity of the Christian faith and to avoid oversimplified or reductionistic views of God and reality.

In summary, having knowledge of the problem of foreknowledge and free will is important for Christians because it helps them to better understand the nature of God, defend their faith, and deepen their faith.

B. The Role of Faith in Resolving the Compatibility Problem

The role of faith in resolving the compatibility problem between divine foreknowledge and human free will is a matter of debate among Christians. Some argue that faith is essential in resolving this problem, while others believe that the problem can be resolved through philosophical and theological arguments alone.

For those who believe that faith is essential, faith provides a way of embracing the mystery of God's foreknowledge and human freedom. They argue that the nature of God is beyond human comprehension and that faith provides a way of accepting this mystery and trusting in the goodness of God.

Others argue that while faith may provide comfort and assurance, it is not necessary to resolve the compatibility problem. They believe that the problem can be resolved through philosophical and theological arguments that show how divine foreknowledge and human freedom can coexist.

Regardless of one's perspective on the role of faith in resolving the compatibility problem, it is widely accepted that the problem of foreknowledge and free will is a deep and complex one, and that both faith and reason are important in understanding and resolving it.

Being Christian apologists, we would have a strong emphasis on the role of faith in resolving the compatibility problem between divine foreknowledge and human free will. We would argue that faith provides a basis for accepting the mystery of this issue, and that it allows individuals to trust in the goodness and sovereignty of God, even if they do not fully understand the relationship between foreknowledge and free will.

We would argue that, while there are philosophical and theological arguments that can be made to reconcile these concepts, faith is ultimately what provides the assurance and comfort that these concepts are compatible. We would point to the example of Molinism, which he supports, as a way of reconciling these concepts through faith.

In our view, the role of faith in resolving the compatibility problem is not to provide a definitive answer, but rather to provide a framework for embracing the mystery of this issue and trusting in God's sovereignty and wisdom. In this way, faith is seen as a key factor in resolving the compatibility problem and maintaining a personal relationship with God.

C. The Relevance of Foreknowledge and Free Will to Personal Faith

The compatibility between divine foreknowledge and human free will is a relevant issue for personal faith, as it raises questions about the nature of God and the freedom of humans.

For many, the concept of divine foreknowledge raises questions about the role of human free will. If God knows everything that will happen in advance, does this mean that human beings have no real freedom to choose their actions? This can lead to feelings of uncertainty and a loss of control over one's life, which can impact one's personal faith.

On the other hand, the belief in human free will raises questions about the nature of God and his knowledge. If humans have the freedom to make choices that are not determined by God, does this mean that God is not all-knowing, or that his knowledge is limited? This can challenge one's beliefs about the omniscience and sovereignty of God.

For many, resolving the compatibility between divine foreknowledge and human free will is a matter of personal faith, as it impacts their understanding of God and their relationship with him. Through faith, they are able to embrace the mystery of this issue and trust in the goodness of God, even if they may not fully understand the relationship between foreknowledge and free will.

Ultimately, the issue of foreknowledge and free will is an important one for personal faith, as it impacts one's beliefs about the nature of God, the freedom of humans, and the relationship between them.

Edward D. Andrews' Easy to Understand Explanation to The Problem of Foreknowledge and Free Will without Predestination

Introduction

The Bible verse John 17:12 states that while Jesus was with his disciples, he kept them in God's name and guarded them, but the son of destruction (Judas Iscariot) perished, so that the scripture would be fulfilled. This raises questions about God's foreknowledge and how it relates to human freedom, especially in the case of Judas Iscariot. This article will explore the topic of God's foreknowledge and free will.

Foreknowledge Does Not Equal Foreordination

Critics argue that by knowing that Judas would betray Jesus, God predestined it to happen, and thus, human freedom is removed. However, the best solution to this problem is to understand that foreknowledge does not equal foreordination. God knows in advance what choices people will freely make, and it is the free decisions of human beings that determine what foreknowledge God has of them, not the reverse.

Foreknowledge and Free Decisions

Foreknowledge does not determine free decisions, but free decisions determine foreknowledge. This can be understood by distinguishing between Chronological Priority and Logical Priority. Chronological priority means that God's knowledge (Event "A") is chronologically prior to the event he foreknows (Event "B"). Logically, the event is prior to God's foreknowledge, meaning the event does not happen because God foreknows it, but God foreknows the event because it will happen.

Foreknowledge as a Foreshadowing

God's foreknowledge can be thought of as a foreshadowing of future events, similar to a shadow on the ground before seeing the person. God's foreknowledge is like an infallible barometer of the future, letting him know what the future will be, but it does not constrain the future in any way.

Foreknowledge and Human Freedom

The presence of God's foreknowledge does not prejudice the occurrence of events, and it does not remove the freedom of the person. For example, if Judas did not betray Jesus, God would not have foreknown the betrayal, and the occurrence of the event would not be affected by the presence of God's foreknowledge.

God's View of the Timeline

God has the ability to see down the timeline, similar to a man in a helicopter looking down on a parade. Just because God has this ability, it does not affect the free will choices of individuals. God has the ability to step into the timeline and alter events, which will create a ripple effect on future events.

Being a Molinist on the foreknowledge without the predestination aspect means that I accept the idea that God has middle knowledge—knowledge of all possible worlds and all possible choices that free agents could make in those worlds—while rejecting the idea of predestination. This perspective holds that God knows in advance what free agents will choose but that these choices are not determined or predetermined by God.

In this view, free agents have the ability to make genuine, uncaused choices, and God's foreknowledge of those choices does not interfere with or constrain the freedom of those choices. This perspective would emphasize the compatibility of divine foreknowledge with human free will while rejecting the idea that God predetermines the choices that people make.

This perspective would also hold that God can use his middle knowledge to guide and influence the choices that people make if he chooses to do so, but that these choices remain genuinely free and uncaused. In this way, God would be able to work all things together for good while still allowing for the freedom and responsibility of human choice.

It is important to note that this perspective, while distinct from traditional Molinism, is still a minority view within the Christian community and may not be widely accepted or understood. Nevertheless, it provides a unique perspective on the relationship between divine foreknowledge and human free will that emphasizes compatibility and freedom.

In conclusion, God's foreknowledge does not equal foreordination, and it does not remove human freedom. God's foreknowledge can be thought of as a foreshadowing of future events, and it does not prejudice the occurrence of events. God has the ability to see down the timeline, but this does not affect the free will choices of individuals.

CHAPTER 3 The Scale of Justice: Understanding Life's Disparities

Navigating Life's Inequities: Beyond Human Perspective

In grappling with the complexities of life's inequities, it is paramount to transcend our finite human perspective and seek understanding from a vantage point that sees both the beginning and end of history. The Scriptures attest to a Creator who is both omniscient and omnipotent, Jehovah, who stands outside the confines of time and human limitation. From this standpoint, life's apparent unfairness is not a product of random chaos or divine neglect but is interwoven into the very fabric of a fallen creation groaning for redemption (Romans 8:22).

When examining life's inequities, one encounters the doctrine of *simple foreknowledge* (πρόγνωσις *prognosis*), which suggests that Jehovah's knowledge of future events does not predetermine them. This knowledge is akin to observing the shadow of an individual approaching a corner; it indicates an impending appearance but does not cause it. It is imperative to consider that the reality of human suffering and the seeming arbitrariness of life's trials are shadows cast forward by the freewill choices made in the garden of Eden and throughout human history.

The Scriptures present Jehovah as a God who *allows* rather than *authors* suffering. For instance, the account of Job reveals a man subjected to severe trials not as punishment or as a result of divine caprice, but as a means to demonstrate fidelity and the limits of Satan's accusations (Job 1-2). Job's experiences serve as a microcosm of the larger conflict concerning God's sovereignty and the question of whether a human will serve Jehovah out of pure motive or merely for gain.

This perspective aligns with Jehovah's declaration that He did not create the earth simply to be empty but to be inhabited by those reflecting His qualities (Isaiah 45:18). The fall in Eden introduced a deviation from the original purpose, yet Jehovah's allowance of suffering since then has not been without profound purpose. The permission of suffering has provided a historical record—a *didactic tableau*—displaying the consequences of rebellion against divine sovereignty and the inadequacy of human rulership devoid of Jehovah's guidance (Jeremiah 10:23).

The Bible affirms the inherent free will endowed to humanity, a quality that allows for genuine love and obedience to Jehovah. However, this gift bears with it the potential for inequity when misused. Human freedom means that the choices of one individual or group can have far-reaching effects on others, sometimes resulting in suffering. This consequence is not a design flaw but a feature of a morally significant universe where choices have real and sometimes painful outcomes. In the Christian Greek Scriptures, *dunamis* (δύναμις) represents power, including the moral freedom to choose one's actions; yet, this freedom does not override Jehovah's ultimate purposes.

The foreknowledge of Jehovah does not eliminate the potentiality of different outcomes. For instance, consider the prophecy concerning Nineveh in the book of Jonah. Jehovah declared its destruction, yet the city's repentance altered the outcome (Jonah 3:10). Thus, foreknowledge encompasses all potentialities, recognizing the fluidity of free will decisions.

The future of humanity, as revealed in Scripture, is not one of an eternally predetermined destiny but of possibilities contingent upon human response to divine grace and sovereignty. The offer of redemption through Christ's ransom sacrifice (Matthew 20:28) and the hope of a restored creation, where suffering will have no place (Revelation 21:4), both hinge upon human participation in Jehovah's purposes.

As for the role of Satan the Devil, his existence is not a myth but a reality that the Bible acknowledges (1 Peter 5:8). His role in the world contributes to suffering, not as a direct cause of every act of evil, but as an influencer toward rebellion against Jehovah. The existence of such a malevolent being introduces a variable in understanding life's inequities—one must account for the spiritual forces at play in the world's suffering.

In the age of human imperfection, Jehovah has not promised absolutes in the sense of a formulaic *quid pro quo*—if one does 'A,' one will invariably receive 'B.' Such a view is inconsistent with the Scriptural portrayal of Jehovah's dealings with humanity. While there are principles that generally lead to blessing or curse, the book of Ecclesiastes candidly addresses the anomalies observed under the sun—the same events befall the righteous and the wicked (Ecclesiastes 9:2). The ultimate guarantees are eschatological, not immediate, bound up in the promises of a new heavens and a new earth wherein righteousness is to dwell (2 Peter 3:13).

In sum, navigating life's inequities requires a panoramic view informed by Scripture. It necessitates the acknowledgment of human freedom, the reality of a spiritual adversary, and the profound scope of Jehovah's foreknowledge and sovereignty. Only within this framework can one begin to understand the moral complexity of a world where divine justice is often deferred, but never denied.

The Role of Free Will in Life's Imbalance

In grappling with the weighty question of why an omnipotent and benevolent God permits suffering, one must explore the intricate relationship between divine sovereignty and human agency. The Bible reveals a God who is omnipresent (Psalm 139:7-12), omniscient (Hebrews 4:13), and omnipotent (Revelation 19:6). Yet, these divine attributes coexist with the genuine freedom granted to human beings—a freedom that is essential to understanding life's disparities.

The Genesis of Free Will

From the beginning, Jehovah imbued humanity with a capacity for moral choice, as seen in the Garden of Eden with the tree of the knowledge of good and evil (Genesis 2:16-17). This freedom, *behirah hofshiyt* in Hebrew, was a pivotal feature of God's design for human beings, made in His image (*tselem*), to reflect His moral qualities. The narrative in Genesis 3 illustrates that Adam and Eve exercised this free will to disobey God's command, which set in motion the cascade of suffering that pervades human history.

The Nature of Foreknowledge

The Greek term *prognōsis*, often translated as "foreknowledge," speaks of God's ability to know in advance what choices human beings will make. This foreknowledge, however, is not causative—it does not constrain or dictate human decisions. Instead, it is descriptive, much like a shadow cast before a person who is about to come around a corner. The shadow is contingent on the person's presence; it does not control their movement. In a similar vein, Jehovah's foreknowledge of future events, including human actions, is contingent on those events actually happening as a result of free will.

God's Sovereignty and Human Suffering

The scriptures do not teach that Jehovah micromanages the universe or predestines every event, a concept known in Greek as *heimarmenē*. Rather, His sovereign will has allowed room for human freedom, even when that freedom results in pain, injustice, or sorrow. It is within this framework of divine permission that the scale of justice tips and tilts on the axis of human choice. It is crucial to distinguish that God allows suffering; He does not author it. In this light, the suffering and evil we observe are, in part, the outworking of human actions free from divine coercion.

The Purpose of Suffering

The existence of suffering serves as a stark reminder of the imperfection of human autonomy apart from divine guidance. The Hebrew Scriptures outline a principle seen in Proverbs 27:12, which says that a prudent person foresees evil and hides himself, but the simple pass on and are punished. Inherent within this wisdom is the acknowledgment that human decisions have consequences. Therefore, suffering, in many respects, is the natural repercussion of choices made contrary to Jehovah's righteous standards.

The Role of the Adversary

One cannot overlook the influence of the adversary, Satan, known in Hebrew as *Ha-Satan*, in contributing to the moral and physical evil in the world. The book of Job (chapters 1-2) presents Satan as a being who challenges the integrity of humans and asserts that they only serve Jehovah for personal gain. In allowing Satan to test Job, God demonstrates that humans can maintain their integrity despite severe suffering, and that such suffering can serve to refine and prove their faith (James 1:2-4).

The Equilibrium of Justice and Mercy

The biblical narrative does not leave humanity without hope in the face of suffering. Jehovah's justice is balanced with His mercy, as demonstrated through the provision of Jesus' ransom sacrifice (Matthew 20:28). It is through this act of divine love that the ultimate resolution to suffering and injustice is provided, ensuring that while we may temporarily endure hardship, there is a promise of restoration and redemption (Acts 3:21).

Humanity's Future Hope

Jehovah's promise for the future—a new heavens and a new earth where righteousness dwells (2 Peter 3:13)—is the concrete hope for rectifying life's disparities. This eschatological vision does not simply offer an escape from the current world but points to a time when God's sovereignty is fully realized, human freedom is exercised in harmony with His will, and suffering as we know it is abolished (Revelation 21:4).

In sum, the scale of justice is unbalanced in this current age not because Jehovah is indifferent or powerless, but because He has granted humans the sobering privilege of free will. The existence of suffering, while perplexing, serves as a pedagogical tool within Jehovah's permissive will. It allows for the demonstration of faith, the refinement of character, and ultimately the vindication of God's sovereignty. By understanding the role of free will in life's imbalance, one can begin to discern the complex interplay between divine providence and human responsibility.

The Illusion of Fairness in a Fallen World

In the pursuit of understanding life's disparities, particularly through the lens of Judeo-Christian scriptures, we encounter the profound and often troubling reality of the human experience: suffering and injustice seem to be woven into the fabric of our existence. At the heart of this perplexity lies the illusion of fairness in a fallen world—a concept that challenges our innate desire for justice and equitable treatment.

The Fall and Its Ripple Effects

To comprehend this illusion, we must start at the beginning, with the concept of the fall of humanity as narrated in Genesis. When Adam and Eve ate from the tree of the knowledge of good and evil, an act often referred to with the Hebrew term *pesha* (transgression), they set into motion a series of events that forever altered the human condition. This original act of disobedience distorted the perfect balance that Jehovah had established, introducing pain, suffering, and death into the world—consequences that continue to ripple across generations.

Human Independence and Suffering

The narratives in the Bible illustrate time and again that human beings often choose paths that lead to suffering. Consider the story of Cain and Abel, where jealousy and anger led to the first murder. Or reflect on the nation of Israel's frequent lapses into idolatry, which brought about cycles of oppression and distress. These historical accounts serve as microcosms of a broader truth: human independence from divine sovereignty frequently results in suffering.

The Sovereignty of God and Human Free Will

The Scriptures assert that Jehovah is sovereign, yet they also affirm human free will—a concept encapsulated in the Greek term *eleutheria* (freedom). This dichotomy can be perplexing: if Jehovah is all-knowing and all-powerful, why does He permit injustice and pain? The Bible does not shy away from this question but rather invites us to explore the dynamics of divine foreknowledge (*prognosis*) and human agency.

God's foreknowledge, akin to the shadow that precedes a person's arrival, suggests that He is aware of future events but does not orchestrate them. Human choices are real and consequential, and while Jehovah knows the end from the beginning, He does not predetermine the moral decisions of individuals. This understanding is crucial, as it maintains human responsibility while acknowledging divine omniscience.

The Problem of Pain as a Consequence

The book of Job exemplifies the struggle to reconcile a just God with the reality of unmerited suffering. Job's plight, while extreme, underscores that righteousness is not a shield against adversity in this current age. His story dispels the notion that suffering is always a direct consequence of personal sin. Rather, it can be a byproduct of living in a world marred by collective fallenness.

The Purpose of Suffering in a Fallen World

It is not that Jehovah designed suffering as a tool for growth, but that in His permissive will, He allows it to accomplish various purposes. The New Testament, particularly in the book of James, speaks of *hupomonē* (endurance) and its refining effect on faith. Suffering has the potential to draw us closer to Jehovah, to depend more fully on Him, and to develop a character more resistant to spiritual corrosion.

Equity in the Eschaton

Looking ahead, biblical prophecy speaks of a time when Jehovah will rectify the imbalances of our present age. The promise of a new heavens and a new earth is a testament to the eventual restoration of divine justice. This future reality will align with Jehovah's initial purpose for humanity—a world without suffering, pain, or death, where fairness is no longer an illusion but a tangible, enduring reality.

In this fallen world, we witness disparities that seem incongruent with the nature of a good and just God. Yet, the Bible provides a framework for understanding these incongruities, positioning them within the context of a larger narrative—one that moves from creation to fall, to redemption, and ultimately to restoration. In the interim, we live in the tension between what is and what will be, guided by the scriptures, trusting in Jehovah's sovereignty, and embracing the freedom He has endowed us with to navigate this life with wisdom and courage.

God's Sovereignty Amidst Earthly Injustice

The concept of God's sovereignty juxtaposed with the reality of earthly injustice is a conundrum that has perplexed scholars and laypeople alike for centuries. The issue often hinges on the fundamental attributes ascribed to Jehovah: omniscience, omnipotence, and omnibenevolence. If God is all-knowing (*pantos ginosko*), all-powerful (*pantokrator*), and all-good (*pas agathosune*), how then can we reconcile the presence of profound and pervasive injustice in the world he has created and continues to govern?

The Divine Perspective of Foreknowledge and Human Autonomy

To begin, we must understand the divine attribute of foreknowledge (*prognosis*), which does not equate to predetermination. In Biblical theology, Jehovah's foreknowledge of future events is not causal; it does not create the reality it perceives. Much like an infallible weather barometer, it records what is to be with unerring accuracy without influencing the weather itself. Similarly, Jehovah's awareness of future injustices does not mean He orchestrates them; rather, He foresees the choices humans will freely make.

In the Biblical narrative, human beings are presented as agents with volition. When Adam and Eve chose to eat from the tree of knowledge of good and evil, Jehovah did not intervene to prevent their decision, despite the foreknowledge of the resulting suffering (Genesis 3:6). The principle at stake was human freedom, and God allowed the consequences of their choices to unfold.

The Reality of Suffering as a Consequence of Human Freedom

Understanding the Biblical perspective on suffering entails recognizing it as a byproduct of the liberty granted to human beings. When Jehovah created man, he was placed in a paradisiacal setting, intended to live in harmony under divine sovereignty (Genesis 1:28). The onset of sin was not a surprise to Jehovah, nor did it derail His original purpose for the earth to be inhabited as expressed in Isaiah 45:18. Instead, it introduced a dimension of existence that allows for suffering and injustice as part of the human experience.

The Scriptures do not shy away from acknowledging the disparities of life. The book of Ecclesiastes discusses the apparent randomness of prosperity and calamity (Ecclesiastes 9:11). The Psalms are replete with laments about the wicked flourishing while the righteous suffer (Psalm 73). Yet, these observations are set against a backdrop of trust in Jehovah's ultimate justice and sovereignty.

The Purpose and Endurance of Injustice in a World Under God's Sovereignty

The existence of evil and suffering has often been cited as an implicit challenge to divine sovereignty. However, within the framework of Biblical theology, the presence of evil is permitted for a time to demonstrate the effects of rebellion against God's sovereignty. This 'object lesson' showcases the futility and inherent corruption of a world system that operates independently of Jehovah's moral governance.

When considering the scope of injustice, the Bible does not gloss over the heart-wrenching impact of such realities. The lamentations of the prophets, the anguished cries of Job, and the weeping of Jesus over Jerusalem all illustrate that Jehovah is not indifferent to human suffering. However, He chooses to work within the parameters of a moral order that respects human freedom while ensuring that His ultimate purposes are achieved.

The Eschatological Resolution of Injustice

Biblical prophecy speaks of a time when Jehovah will address all injustices. The visions in Daniel and Revelation point to the establishment of God's Kingdom, where righteousness dwells and suffering is no more (Daniel 2:44; Revelation 21:3-4). The promise of a 'new heavens and a new earth' is not a metaphorical aspiration but a literal restoration of divine order (2 Peter 3:13).

In this future state, the Bible speaks of the resurrection, a time when those who have suffered unjustly will be vindicated and restored (John 5:28-29). This hope reflects a fundamental aspect of God's character: He is a God of justice, and His sovereignty ensures that justice will ultimately prevail.

Conclusion

In summary, Jehovah's sovereignty does not negate human freedom, nor does it remove the moral and natural consequences of human actions. While He foreknows the course that humanity will take, He does not orchestrate the evil that results from human choices. Instead, He permits it for a time, to demonstrate the fruitage of a world alienated from His sovereignty. But with Jehovah, justice is not an abstract concept; it is an assured outcome, rooted in His immutable character. As we grapple with life's disparities, we do so with the knowledge that Jehovah is both sovereign and just, and that His justice will restore all things in His appointed time.

CHAPTER 4 Divine Intervention: Expectations vs. Reality

The Myth of Constant Divine Rescue

In grappling with the enigma of Jehovah's intervention in human affairs, we encounter the myth of constant divine rescue—a belief deeply ingrained in some religious circles. This myth posits that as a sign of His goodness and power, God will always step in to prevent suffering and to safeguard His followers from the perils of life. Yet, the reality as presented in the Scriptures diverges from this perception. The expectation of constant divine rescue is confronted by the biblical narrative, which shows that while Jehovah is certainly capable of miraculous deliverance, He does not intervene in every instance of human suffering or adversity.

To understand the expectations versus the reality of divine intervention, we must examine the principle of *simple foreknowledge*. This concept reflects the understanding that Jehovah knows all things, inclusive of future events (*prognōsis*), but His knowledge does not predetermine those events. Free will operates within the purview of divine omniscience, allowing for human actions to unfold freely even though they are fully known by God ahead of time.

Consider the account of Job. Job's sufferings were not the result of a lack of divine foresight or concern. Rather, they provided a vivid demonstration of the distinction between God's foreknowledge and His permissive will. Jehovah knew the afflictions Job would face, yet He allowed them to proceed—not as a determinant but as a part of the broader cosmic conflict between good and evil, highlighting the integrity of a faithful individual under trial.

Similarly, the life of Jesus Christ gives insight into the intersection of divine foreknowledge and human experience. Predicted in detail through prophecies, Christ's sufferings were foreknown (*proetoimazō*), yet they occurred due to human actions and decisions. Jehovah's foreknowledge did not necessitate the betrayal by Judas or the denial by Peter; these were actions freely chosen by men, yet known by God in advance.

Furthermore, the writings of the apostle Paul often reflect on the purpose and meaning behind suffering. For instance, in Romans 5:3-4, Paul speaks of suffering producing perseverance, character, and hope, not as predetermined outcomes but as potentialities that can arise through the human response to trials in faith.

When pondering the question of why Jehovah allows suffering if He is good, one must consider the nature of the world post-Eden. The fall of humanity introduced imperfection and death into what was designed to be a perfect human experience on earth. Jehovah's allowance of suffering is not indicative of a flaw in His character but reveals His commitment to human freedom and the ultimate resolution of moral and spiritual issues raised by rebellion against His sovereignty.

The Scriptural narrative presents Jehovah as a God who is deeply concerned with human suffering, yet who often chooses not to intervene miraculously to prevent it. This is not due to a lack of power or compassion but is in keeping with His purpose for humanity and the respect for the moral agency He has granted. For example, *Psalm 73* poetically explores the tension felt by the psalmist when observing the prosperity of the wicked compared to the suffering of the righteous. The resolution comes in the recognition of ultimate justice and divine sovereignty.

In the context of the Christian Greek Scriptures, the term *thlipsis* (tribulation) is used to describe the challenges faced by believers. The early Christian community, as chronicled in Acts and the Epistles, faced persecution and suffering not as signs of divine abandonment but as opportunities to demonstrate faithfulness and as arenas where divine strength was made perfect in human weakness (*astheneia*).

In conclusion, the myth of constant divine rescue is dispelled by the testimony of the Scriptures, which show that while Jehovah is intimately aware of human suffering and capable of intervention, He does not provide a shield against every trial. Instead, He offers His presence, the comfort of His Spirit, and the hope of a future where justice will be established, and suffering will be no more. The ultimate divine intervention was the sacrifice of Jesus Christ, which addresses the root of human suffering—sin and death. Through Christ, Jehovah provides the means for redemption and the assurance of His kingdom, where His will shall be done on earth as it is in heaven, bringing an end to suffering and death. The expectation of constant divine rescue may not align with reality, but the hope of God's ultimate deliverance is a firm assurance for those who trust in His promises.

Faithfulness and the Reality of Life's Struggles

The intersection of divine omniscience and human suffering is a profound topic that has perplexed theologians, philosophers, and believers throughout the centuries. The challenge often lies in reconciling the reality of life's struggles with the faithful character of Jehovah, who is depicted in the Scriptures as both all-knowing and inherently good. The biblical narrative does not shy away from these tensions; rather, it provides a framework for understanding them.

The Complexity of Divine Foreknowledge

Divine foreknowledge (*prognōsis* in Greek) is the concept that Jehovah is aware of all things that will occur, without directly causing them. This knowledge is perfect and complete, encompassing not only the actualities of history but also the possibilities—the myriad choices each individual may make. The idea that Jehovah has this kind of knowledge does not negate human freedom; it simply acknowledges His capacity to know our decisions before we make them.

Consider the analogy of an experienced chess player who can predict the moves of a novice. The skilled player's anticipation of the novice's moves does not cause those moves to occur; the novice still retains the freedom to make any legal move on the board. Similarly, Jehovah's foreknowledge of our decisions does not cause those decisions. We are like the novice chess player, with the freedom to make our moves, yet those moves are known by Jehovah before we make them.

Human Suffering and Divine Purpose

It is essential to recognize that Jehovah did not create suffering as a means to an end. The occurrence of pain and hardship is a result of human fallibility and the subsequent distancing from Jehovah's intended purpose for humanity, not a tool fashioned by His hand. When reflecting on texts such as Romans 5:3-4, which speaks of suffering producing perseverance, character, and hope, it is not that Jehovah designs suffering for these ends, but rather that He can use such circumstances to refine those who remain faithful to Him.

In the Hebrew Scriptures, the term *yissurin*, often translated as "disciplines" or "sufferings," conveys the reality that the children of Israel faced many hardships. However, through these experiences, Jehovah taught them dependence on His guidance rather than on their understanding or strength, as seen in Proverbs 3:5-6.

The Misconception of Destiny and the Reality of Choice

Contrary to fatalistic doctrines, the Bible underscores the role of human choice and its consequences. Jehovah sets before us life and death, blessing and cursing, and encourages us to choose life, as stated in Deuteronomy 30:19. The concept of destiny implies a predetermined outcome that is unchangeable, but the biblical narrative reveals a God who responds to human decisions in real time, illustrating a dynamic relationship rather than a static script.

When we consider the accounts of individuals like King Saul and David, we see two different trajectories shaped by their choices. Saul, chosen by Jehovah and anointed as king, later turned away from following Jehovah's commands, leading to his downfall (1 Samuel 15). David, on the other hand, despite his serious sins, sought forgiveness and endeavored to align his will with Jehovah's, which influenced the course of his life (Psalms 51).

The Original Plan and Human Redemption

In the Genesis account, Jehovah's purpose for the earth was clear—to be filled with a perfect human family living in harmony with His will (Genesis 1:28). Even after the entrance of sin, Jehovah's purpose did not waver. He set in motion a plan of redemption through the ransom sacrifice of Jesus Christ, offering a means for humanity to be restored to its original purpose.

The concept of resurrection is critical to understanding Jehovah's response to suffering. In the New Testament, the Greek word *anastasis*, meaning "raising up" or "standing up again," is used to describe this hope. It reflects Jehovah's power to reverse the effects of sin and death, ultimately fulfilling His original intention for the earth.

The Harsh Reality of a Fallen World

In a world marked by sin and imperfection, suffering is pervasive, and the righteous are not exempt from trials. The book of Job offers a poignant example. Job was a man of faithfulness, yet he experienced profound suffering. It was not a punishment from Jehovah but rather a test of faith, which Job passed by maintaining his integrity (Job 2:3). The Psalms also echo this theme, often lamenting the presence of evil and suffering while simultaneously expressing trust in Jehovah's justice and care (Psalms 37:28-29).

The Expectation of Divine Intervention

While it is true that Jehovah has, at times, intervened miraculously in human affairs, such interventions are exceptions rather than norms. The Scriptures reveal a God who is patient, allowing time for humans to return to Him, and who often works through natural means and human agency rather than overt miracles. It is a mistake to presume that faithfulness will always result in immediate divine intervention to alleviate suffering. Instead, Jehovah provides us with the strength to endure and the hope of a future where suffering will no longer exist (Revelation 21:4).

In summary, divine omniscience and human suffering coexist within the biblical framework that acknowledges Jehovah's complete knowledge, the reality of human choice, and the hope of redemption. Life's struggles, though challenging, are seen as opportunities for growth and reminders of our need for reliance on Jehovah's guidance and the hope of His promises.

Understanding the Limits of God's Earthly Intervention

The question of divine intervention and the limits thereof is one that has perplexed theologians, scholars, and laypeople alike. To approach this topic, one must first consider the nature of Jehovah's omniscience—His all-knowing character. In the Scriptures, Jehovah's knowledge is presented as exhaustive and all-encompassing. The Hebrew word for knowledge, *da'at*, and the Greek *gnosis*, suggest a deep, intimate understanding that goes beyond mere awareness. However, this divine attribute does not negate human freedom nor does it imply that Jehovah actively determines every event on earth.

The role of divine intervention must be understood within the framework of Jehovah's sovereignty and the allowance for human autonomy. Throughout the Bible, there are numerous examples of Jehovah stepping into the human story to guide, correct, or deliver. Yet, these instances do not constitute a pattern whereby one can predict or expect intervention in every circumstance. Consider the Israelites' exodus from Egypt, where Jehovah intervened in a dramatic and powerful way through plagues, parting the Red Sea, and the ultimate delivery into the Promised Land. This level of divine action sets a precedent for Jehovah's ability to intervene but does not establish an obligation for Him to do so in every situation.

Moving into the New Testament, the Greek word *dunamis* (power) is often associated with miraculous acts or divine intervention. Jesus' ministry was marked by *dunamis*, from healing the sick to feeding the multitudes. Yet, even within His ministry, Jesus did not heal every sick person in Israel, nor did He provide miraculous deliverance for all who suffered under Roman oppression. These miracles were signs pointing to His divine authority and kingdom, not a model for uninterrupted divine intervention.

In grappling with the reality of suffering and the expectation of divine intervention, one must also consider the concept of *providence*—Jehovah's ongoing relationship with His creation. Providence does not imply that Jehovah orchestrates every event but suggests that He is continuously at work in the world, guiding and sustaining according to His will and purpose. For instance, when Paul was shipwrecked on Malta in Acts 28, one could see Jehovah's providential hand at work, using the situation for His purposes, even though the initial event was not directly caused by divine action.

Foreknowledge is another key aspect when discussing the limits of divine intervention. Jehovah, being outside of time, knows the end from the beginning, as stated in Isaiah 46:10. However, His foreknowledge does not necessitate predestination of every event. Jehovah's knowing an event will occur is not the same as causing it to happen. Instead, this knowledge allows for a comprehensive understanding of all possible outcomes without infringing on human freedom. The reality of foreknowledge should not lead to fatalism but to a reassurance that Jehovah is never surprised or unprepared, and His purposes will ultimately be fulfilled.

In addressing the presence of evil and suffering, one cannot ignore the biblical teaching on *theodicy*—the justice of Jehovah in the face of evil. The reality of suffering and the apparent lack of intervention must be viewed within the context of the larger biblical narrative. The Bible asserts that Jehovah is good and just, and that evil entered the world through human rebellion (Genesis 3). The existence of suffering is not an indication of Jehovah's indifference but a consequence of living in a fallen world where human beings have been granted the dignity of choice.

This framework does not mean that Jehovah is disengaged from human suffering. Scriptures like Psalm 34:18, which says Jehovah is close to the brokenhearted, offer comfort that He is intimately aware of human pain and responds in ways that are not always visible or immediate. The ultimate act of intervention was sending Jesus Christ to redeem humankind, which showcases Jehovah's commitment to dealing with the problem of sin and suffering. The cross stands as a concrete example of Jehovah's willingness to enter into human suffering to bring about redemption and hope.

In conclusion, the limits of God's earthly intervention cannot be encapsulated by human expectations or desires.

Jehovah is sovereign, and His ways are higher than our ways (Isaiah 55:9). He intervenes according to His wisdom and purposes, which often transcend human understanding. Believers are called to trust in Jehovah's goodness and sovereignty, even when His intervention does not align with human expectations. The reality of suffering and the anticipation of divine intervention must be held in tension with the hope of the resurrection and the promise of a future where Jehovah will wipe away every tear and suffering will be no more.

The Purpose Behind Unanswered Prayers

In addressing the profound and often troubling question of why some prayers seem to go unanswered, we must consider the nature of prayer itself and its role within the divine-human relationship. Prayer, in its essence, is communication with the Divine, a conduit through which human beings express their desires, hopes, and confessions. However, the outcome of prayer is not always in alignment with the petitioner's requests. This divergence between human expectation and divine response is rooted in the disparity between human will and the will of Jehovah.

Prayer and Divine Will

The scriptures inform us that prayers aligned with Jehovah's will are the ones that pierce the heavens and find a response (1 John 5:14). The Greek word for "will" is θέλημα (*thelema*), which indicates God's desire or purpose. It is imperative to understand that Jehovah is sovereign, and His plans transcend human understanding (Isaiah 55:8-9). When prayers seem unanswered, it might be that they are not congruent with His *thelema*. For instance, James 4:3

speaks of asking amiss, with wrong motives, which will not yield Jehovah's blessing.

Human Expectations in Prayer

Humans often approach prayer with specific expectations: healing from illness, resolution of a conflict, or prevention of a calamity. They might pray with the word δύναμις (*dunamis*), meaning "power," in mind, hoping for a powerful intervention that changes their circumstances. However, the reality is that Jehovah's power is not a cosmic force at our beck and call but is exercised in harmony with His purposes and the ultimate benefit of His creation.

The Intersection of Foreknowledge and Prayer

Understanding Jehovah's πρόγνωσις (*prognosis*), or foreknowledge, is crucial here. Foreknowledge does not equate to predestination. Jehovah, in His omniscience, knows the countless potential outcomes of our free will decisions. Yet, this foreknowledge does not impinge upon human freedom. Rather, it is akin to an infallible forecaster that accurately understands the future's shape based on present choices.

Learning Through Unanswered Prayers

Unanswered prayers, therefore, can be pedagogical. They teach us about the limits of our autonomy and the need to align ourselves with Jehovah's sovereignty. As we navigate through the outcomes of our free will under Jehovah's permissive will, we encounter a range of experiences that teach us about reliance, humility, and the transient nature of our existence. The book of Ecclesiastes often reflects on the vaporous quality of life (הֶבֶל *hevel*), which underscores our dependence on Jehovah for meaning and purpose.

The Object Lesson of Suffering

Suffering, a result of human rebellion and the imperfection that ensued, serves as an object lesson. Jehovah did not design suffering, but He permits it within His permissive will. This allowance serves to demonstrate the flaws in human independence and the necessity of divine guidance and sovereignty. Jehovah's allowance of suffering is not without purpose but is part of the greater narrative that culminates in redemption and restoration.

The Ultimate Hope Beyond Unanswered Prayers

The Bible presents a vision of hope beyond the present suffering and seemingly unanswered prayers. This hope is rooted in the assurance of Jehovah's unfailing promises and the ultimate restoration of all things. The promise of a new heavens and a new earth (Revelation 21:1) is the culmination of Jehovah's redemptive plan, a plan that transcends the immediate and often myopic desires expressed in human prayers.

In this context, unanswered prayers serve a dual purpose. They refine our understanding and expectations of prayer, drawing us closer to Jehovah's heart, and they remind us that our current sufferings are temporary when set against the backdrop of Jehovah's eternal plan. They are not denials but redirections towards a deeper trust in Jehovah and His salvific work through Jesus Christ. This divine narrative weaves through history, guiding humanity toward an ultimate reality where pain and suffering have no place, and where Jehovah's purposes, in their fullness, are realized.

In sum, the purpose behind unanswered prayers is to lead us into deeper communion with Jehovah, aligning our will with His and teaching us to trust in His ultimate sovereignty and goodness. Unanswered prayers are not a divine oversight or a celestial malfunction but are, in fact, a part of Jehovah's intricate design, a design that guides us toward the ultimate reality of His will done "on earth as it is in heaven" (Matthew 6:10).

CHAPTER 5 The Adversary Unveiled: Acknowledging Satan's Role

The Reality of Evil Personified

In the discourse of theodicy, the acknowledgment of Satan as a personal, active agent of evil is indispensable. The Scriptures delineate Satan, not as an abstract concept or a mere symbol of human malfeasance but as a concrete, malevolent being with a will, intelligence, and influence. This reality bears upon the matter of divine foreknowledge and human suffering in a manner that is both profound and complex.

The portrayal of Satan begins in the Hebrew Bible, with terms like *Satan* (שָׂטָן, *satān*), meaning adversary or accuser, and carries into the New Testament with Greek terminology like *Diabolos* (Διάβολος, *Diabolos*), commonly translated as "devil," which means slanderer or accuser. From the onset, the biblical narrative does not shy away from presenting a cosmic conflict, an unseen war that spills into human history.

Satan's Role in Human Affliction

The Book of Job is one of the earliest and most vivid depictions of Satan's activity within human affairs. Here, *Satan* appears in the heavenly court as the accuser, challenging the integrity of Job's piety and suggesting that his faithfulness is merely a byproduct of divine protection and blessing. Jehovah permits *Satan* to afflict Job, thus setting the stage for an exploration of righteousness, suffering, and divine justice. This narrative establishes an important principle: Satan instigates suffering, but it is God who sets the parameters of the trial and remains sovereign over the outcome.

In the New Testament, Satan's influence expands. He is described as "the god of this age" (2 Corinthians 4:4) and "the ruler of the kingdom of the air" (Ephesians 2:2), signifying a pervasive, albeit temporary, dominion over the earth. The Gospels present Jesus Himself as recognizing and confronting Satan's role in causing suffering and corruption, embodying divine authority over the forces of evil. The temptation of Jesus (Matthew 4:1-11; Luke 4:1-13) demonstrates Satan's real and personal opposition to God's redemptive plan, and Jesus' resistance exemplifies the proper response to such malevolence.

Theological Implications of a Personal Evil

Understanding Satan as a personal being rather than a mere allegory or impersonal force has significant theological implications. It clarifies the nature of the spiritual struggle and provides a framework for understanding the complex interplay between divine sovereignty and human agency. Satan's existence does not diminish God's power or His goodness; instead, it accentuates the reality of free will and the consequential nature of rebellion against divine authority.

Satan's role in human suffering is thus seen not as a challenge to God's omnipotence but as a permitted part of the narrative that God is unfolding. Just as God foreknows the outcome of the cosmic conflict without predetermining every specific choice within it, He allows for Satan's actions within the constraints of His sovereign will. This distinction between foreknowledge and predestination is crucial, for it safeguards human responsibility and the authenticity of moral choices.

Satan and the Free Will Defense

The recognition of Satan as an active adversary offers substance to the free will defense in the problem of evil. It posits that much of the suffering in the world is attributable to the misuse of free will by created beings, both human and angelic. As Satan exercises his free will in opposition to Jehovah, so too do humans in their personal decisions to rebel or conform to divine standards.

However, this view does not absolve God of His creatorship over all beings, including Satan. The divine allowance for Satan's temporary role in the world is an expression of God's patient and redemptive plan, which culminates in the ultimate defeat of evil and restoration of all things. The presence of Satan and the reality of evil serve as the dark backdrop against which the luminescence of God's love, justice, and mercy are most vividly displayed.

Satan's Defeat and Eschatological Hope

Finally, any discussion of Satan must inevitably lead to the hope laid out in the prophetic scriptures. The Bible portrays a future in which Satan's defeat is certain and complete. Revelation 20:10 speaks of the devil being thrown into the lake of fire, signaling an end to his influence and the cessation of the suffering he has caused. This eschatological vision presents not just the end of an adversary but the restoration of the intended harmony between God, humanity, and creation.

In sum, the acknowledgment of Satan's role in human suffering adds depth to the discussion of theodicy and the question posed by the book title, "If God is Good: Why Does God Allow Suffering?" It presents the Christian narrative not as a simplistic story of an omnipotent deity orchestrating a world without true freedom but as a complex and profound account of love, judgment, redemption, and hope amid the very real struggle against a personal embodiment of evil.

Satan's Influence and the Battle for Good

In the grand narrative of the Bible, the figure of Satan stands as the chief adversary to both God and humanity. His role in the cosmic struggle between good and evil is pivotal, and understanding his influence is crucial to comprehending why God permits suffering.

The Origin and Fall of Satan

To grasp Satan's influence, we must begin with his origin. Isaiah 14:12-15 and Ezekiel 28:12-17, while primarily addressed to the kings of Babylon and Tyre, respectively, have been interpreted by some scholars as alluding to the figure of Satan, describing his fall from a position of prominence. These passages, rich with metaphor, suggest a being who, due to pride and rebellion, was cast down from a high position. In the Hebrew Bible, the term *helel* (הֵילֵל), often translated as "morning star" or "Lucifer" in Latin, is used in Isaiah, whereas Ezekiel refers to a cherub who was in Eden. These texts, while not explicit about the Devil's origins, when combined with the New Testament revelation, paint a picture of a created being who turned against his Creator.

Satan's Role in Human Affairs

Satan's influence extends to the human realm, where he is seen as a tempter, accuser, and deceiver. In the Garden of Eden narrative (Genesis 3), Satan, in the form of a serpent (*nahash*, נָחָשׁ), tempts Eve by questioning God's command and suggesting God is withholding good from her and Adam. This act introduces sin and suffering into the human experience, highlighting Satan's role in fostering disobedience against God.

The Character and Methods of Satan

In the New Testament, Satan is called *diabolos* (διάβολος), meaning "slanderer" or "accuser." He is depicted as the ruler of this world's systems (John 12:31), and his methods are multifaceted. For instance, in the parable of the sower, Jesus explains that Satan snatches away the word from people's hearts (Luke 8:12). In 2 Corinthians 4:4, he is described as the god of this age who blinds the minds of unbelievers. These descriptions emphasize his role in hindering people from grasping the truth of the Gospel, thereby extending the reach of suffering and estrangement from God.

The Reality of Spiritual Warfare

The influence of Satan is not merely a symbolic or mythological representation of evil. Ephesians 6:12 speaks of our struggle not against flesh and blood, but against spiritual forces of evil. The term *palē* (πάλη) refers to a wrestling match, indicating a close, intense struggle.

Christians are called to be aware of the spiritual battle that rages and to equip themselves with spiritual armor (Ephesians 6:13-17).

Satan's Influence on Suffering

The book of Job is perhaps the most direct biblical exploration of the relationship between Satan and human suffering. Satan challenges Job's integrity, suggesting that his righteousness is merely due to God's protection and blessings (Job 1:9-11). God permits Satan to afflict Job, leading to immense suffering. This account reveals Satan's accusatory role and suggests that while God allows Satan a certain degree of influence, it is not without limits and ultimate purpose.

The Accusation and Redemption Paradigm

In Revelation 12:10, Satan is called the accuser of the brethren, who accuses them day and night. This continuous accusation aligns with the suffering of the faithful, as their trials are often a result of such spiritual opposition. However, the same passage proclaims the defeat of the accuser through the blood of the Lamb, showing that while Satan's influence is significant, it is ultimately overpowered by Christ's redemptive work.

God's Sovereignty and Satan's Boundaries

The influence of Satan is formidable but not ultimate. Job's narrative demonstrates that Satan operates only within the boundaries permitted by God (Job 1:12). The concept of *dunamis* (δύναμις), often translated as "power" or "strength," is attributed to God alone in its ultimate sense.

Satan's power is derivative and limited when compared to the sovereignty of Jehovah.

The Free Will Aspect in the Cosmic Conflict

Human beings are central to the conflict between good and evil. God's foreknowledge (*prognōsis*, πρόγνωσις) of future events does not negate human freedom or responsibility. It's not that God has pre-written a script that creation follows blindly, but rather He is aware of all possible outcomes. In allowing for human freedom, God permits Satan's influence as a factor in the moral and spiritual development of humanity. God's foreknowledge of human decisions and Satan's activities does not cause them but rather anticipates them within His eternal plan.

The End of Satan's Influence

The Bible indicates a time when Satan's influence will be decisively ended. Revelation 20:10 describes Satan's final destiny in the lake of fire, an image symbolizing complete and eternal destruction. This event will eliminate suffering and evil, restoring God's intended order.

Satan's influence is a significant but temporary part of the broader narrative of the Bible. It serves as a backdrop to the drama of human salvation and the vindication of God's character and government. While God permits Satan to operate within certain limits, the biblical assurance is that this malevolent influence will not last forever, and that God, in His wisdom, will bring all things to a righteous conclusion.

Demystifying the Devil: Scripture's Testimony

In seeking to understand the role of the adversary within the context of God's goodness and the existence of suffering, it is imperative to delve deeply into the biblical testimony about Satan. This exploration is not to amplify his importance, but to clarify his role within the divine narrative and the human experience.

Satan's Origins and Nature

Scripture does not provide a comprehensive biography of Satan, but it offers glimpses into his nature and function. The Hebrew Bible introduces him as *ha-satan* (הַשָּׂטָן), meaning "the accuser" or "the adversary." The term itself is not a proper name but a title, depicting his role as an opposer. His first notable appearance in the book of Job (Job 1:6-12) presents him as a being who challenges the integrity of humans, suggesting that their faithfulness is merely a product of divine blessing. This character attributes to Satan an interest in the moral and spiritual state of humanity, with a particular focus on their loyalty to Jehovah.

In the New Testament, the Greek term *diabolos* (διάβολος), translated as "devil," means "slanderer" or "accuser." This title indicates his role as one who defames and misrepresents the character of individuals before God. The epistle of 1 Peter 5:8 vividly describes him as "a roaring lion, walking about, seeking whom he may devour," which symbolically portrays his destructive intentions.

Satan's Fall and Rebellion

While the specifics are not exhaustively detailed in the Bible, certain passages suggest a pre-human fall from a position of honor. Isaiah 14:12-15 and Ezekiel 28:12-17, often interpreted as references to human kings, are also seen by some as alluding to the fall of Satan. The imagery used in these passages—falling from heaven, being cast down to the earth—parallels the New Testament descriptions of a spiritual being who rebelled against God.

The New Testament solidifies the narrative of Satan's fall. Luke 10:18 recounts Jesus' words, "I beheld Satan as lightning fall from heaven," which metaphorically speaks of a swift and irreversible downfall. This downfall is the result of rebellion, a conscious decision to oppose God's sovereignty, which introduces a state of moral and spiritual corruption.

Satan's Activities and Influence

The scriptural accounts of Satan's activities are multifaceted. He is depicted as one who tempts (Matthew 4:1-11), deceives (Revelation 12:9), and blinds the minds of the unbelieving (2 Corinthians 4:4). These actions portray an entity that is actively working to thwart God's purposes and lead humanity astray.

The temptation of Jesus in the wilderness is a poignant example of Satan's tactics. He uses scripture (Psalm 91:11-12) to try and manipulate Jesus, showing a perverted application of God's Word for his own ends. This incident reveals Satan's awareness of scripture and his willingness to distort it to achieve his goals.

Satan and Human Suffering

While Satan is portrayed as a significant figure in the realm of spiritual opposition, it is crucial to maintain a balanced perspective. His ability to influence human affairs and cause suffering is significant but not sovereign. The book of Job demonstrates that while Satan can be a catalyst for suffering, he operates under divine permission (Job 1:12). This indicates that his power is not autonomous but is allowed within the parameters set by God for reasons that are ultimately connected to God's overarching plan and human freedom.

In the Christian Greek Scriptures, particularly in the epistles of John, Satan is described as "the ruler of this world" (John 12:31). This rulership, however, is not an ultimate or uncontestable authority but is subject to the sovereignty of God and the redemptive work of Christ.

Foreknowledge and Satan's Role

The interplay between divine foreknowledge and the activities of Satan is a subject of profound mystery. While God in His omniscience foreknows all that will occur, this foreknowledge does not equate to causation. Jehovah's knowledge of Satan's choices and actions does not compel them; rather, He foresees them in His infinite awareness of all realities. God's foreknowledge is impeccably accurate, much like the previously mentioned infallible barometer. It detects and reflects reality but does not dictate or generate it.

The book of Revelation offers a panoramic view of God's foreknowledge regarding Satan's end. Though Satan is active now, his doom is certain, as prophesied in Revelation 20:10, where he will be thrown into the lake of fire—symbolic of total destruction and the cessation of his influence.

Conclusion Within the Confines of Scripture's Testimony

To understand Satan's role in the context of God's sovereignty and the existence of suffering, one must look to the complete counsel of scripture. It portrays an adversary whose influence, though real and destructive, is neither ultimate nor beyond the purview of Jehovah's redemptive plan. Satan's existence and actions serve as a backdrop against which the themes of free will, divine justice, and redemption unfold in the biblical narrative. His role is significant but is ultimately bounded by the purposes and power of the Almighty.

The Existential Threat: Combatting Spiritual Deception

In the realm of spiritual warfare, the Bible presents the concept of *spiritual deception* as a pervasive and existential threat. Satan, known in Hebrew as הַשָּׂטָן (*ha-satan*), meaning "the accuser," and in Greek as Σατανᾶς (*Satanas*), operates primarily as a deceiver whose primary objective is to lead humanity away from the truth of Jehovah and into error and sin. This chapter will explore the multifaceted role that Satan plays in spiritual deception and the tools that believers have at their disposal to combat this formidable adversary.

In the Scriptures, the character of Satan is unveiled as one who masquerades as an "angel of light" (2 Corinthians 11:14). The term φωσφόρος (*phosphoros*), often used to describe a light-bearer, is illustrative of the deceptive nature of Satan—he does not present himself as the source of darkness that he is, but rather as a beacon of false enlightenment. This deception is a potent threat because it is not always overtly evil; it often appears as a subtle twist on the truth, making it difficult to discern and resist.

One of the primary examples of Satan's deceptive tactics can be seen in the narrative of the Garden of Eden. The serpent (Genesis 3:1), a manifestation of Satan, did not forcefully persuade Eve to eat the forbidden fruit. Instead, he sowed seeds of doubt about Jehovah's word and His motives, asking, "Did God really say...?" (Genesis 3:1). This question highlights a key strategy of the adversary: to challenge the veracity of Jehovah's word and thus undermine trust in Him. The Hebrew verb used, *sha'al*, implies not just a question but a challenge—aiming to erode certainty and instill skepticism.

Furthermore, the adversary's influence is not limited to the spiritual realm but extends to the physical world, affecting individuals and systems. For instance, in the book of Job, Satan is granted permission to afflict Job to test his integrity. The Hebrew term שָׂטָן (*satan*) in Job 1:6 is not merely a proper noun but also a title, denoting one who opposes or obstructs. Job's severe trials, permitted by Jehovah, are demonstrative of the adversarial challenges believers may face, emphasizing the necessity for steadfast faith and trust in Jehovah's ultimate justice and goodness.

The New Testament Greek text also warns believers about the schemes (μεθοδεία *methodeia*) of the Devil (Ephesians 6:11). This term denotes craftiness and deceit— tactical plans laid out with the intention to ensnare. It is a reminder that the battle believers engage in is not one of brute force, but rather of cunning and strategy, necessitating the full armor of God for defense.

In understanding the foreknowledge of Jehovah, it is essential to realize that Jehovah's omniscience, including His foreknowledge, does not negate human freedom nor does it predetermine the deceptive work of Satan. Just as God foreknew the fall of humankind, He also foresaw the redemption that would be made possible through the sacrifice of Jesus Christ. This foreknowledge, exemplified by the Greek term πρόγνωσις (*prognosis*), does not cause the events that transpire in the temporal realm but rather acknowledges their certainty in the divine economy. Jehovah's allowance of suffering and evil, including that perpetrated by the adversary, ultimately serves to highlight the justness of His sovereignty and the necessity of living in harmony with His will, as opposed to under the guidance of the adversary.

To combat spiritual deception, believers are urged to hold fast to the *logos*, the Word of God, which is sharper than any two-edged sword (Hebrews 4:12). The term λόγος (*logos*) here signifies more than mere words; it represents the divine truth, the ultimate revelation of Jehovah's will, embodied in the person of Jesus Christ and inscribed in the Scriptures. It is through a deep understanding and application of this Word that believers can discern the lies of the adversary and remain firm in their commitment to the truth.

The historical manifestation of Jesus Christ, whose life and teachings are recorded in the Greek Scriptures, stands as a testament to Jehovah's sovereignty over the deceptive works of the adversary. Through His ministry, Jesus exposed the lies of the adversary, cast out demons, and illuminated the path to reconciliation with Jehovah. The Greek term ἀλήθεια (*aletheia*), truth, is frequently used in the New Testament to describe both the nature of Christ and the divine reality He came to reveal, providing a stark contrast to the falsehoods propagated by the adversary.

In conclusion, the threat posed by Satan in spiritual deception is both complex and challenging. It is an ongoing struggle that requires vigilance, knowledge of the Scriptures, and reliance on Jehovah. Believers must equip themselves with the truth, discern the subtleties of the adversary's lies, and anchor their hope in the redemptive work of Christ. In doing so, they will not only defend themselves against deception but will also stand as beacons of truth in a world often shrouded in spiritual darkness.

CHAPTER 6 Promises and Perseverance: Navigating Imperfection with God

Conditional Promises: Misconceptions and Clarifications

In a world marred by imperfection and suffering, the understanding of God's promises becomes a beacon of hope for many. However, misconceptions abound regarding the nature and application of these promises. The key to navigating such confusion lies in a thorough comprehension of the *conditional* nature of many of God's assurances to humanity.

The Nature of Divine Conditions

Throughout the Scriptures, Jehovah has extended promises that are not blanket guarantees but are instead contingent upon human response and obedience. Consider the ancient Israelites; their entrance and continued residence in the Promised Land were conditional upon their obedience to God's laws (Deuteronomy 28:1-68). The Hebrew term *shama*, meaning to "hear" or "obey," illustrates the expectation of a responsive action to divine instruction, which in turn brings about the fulfillment of a promise.

Free Will and Divine Foreknowledge

The concept of free will is critical when discussing conditional promises. The Scriptures teach that humans have the freedom to choose their actions (Deuteronomy 30:19). This freedom does not negate the reality of divine foreknowledge, represented in the Greek New Testament by terms like *prognōsis*, meaning "foreknowledge." Jehovah, by His very nature, is aware of all potential outcomes of free will decisions. His foreknowledge, akin to an infallible barometer, does not constrain human choices but rather anticipates them in all their variability.

Misinterpretation of Promises

Misinterpretation of biblical promises often arises from reading them in isolation, without the larger biblical context. For instance, *Jeremiah 29:11* is frequently cited as a universal promise for personal prosperity. Yet, in its context, this verse was a specific promise to the exiled nation of Israel and included the nation's expected action of seeking Jehovah with their whole heart.

The Purpose Behind the Promises

The purpose behind God's conditional promises is multifaceted. They are not designed to entrap or set up humanity for failure but to encourage a relationship built on trust, obedience, and mutual commitment. Jehovah's promises are invitations to experience His faithfulness and to cultivate qualities pleasing to Him, such as faith and endurance. The Greek term *hypomonē*, often translated as "endurance," conveys the idea of remaining under a burden. This endurance is developed and tested through the trials that come despite the presence of divine promises.

Perseverance in the Face of Imperfection

Human imperfection necessitates perseverance. The epistle of James encourages believers to let endurance complete its work so that they may be mature and complete (James 1:4). This maturation process happens as believers navigate the complexities of a fallen world, holding on to God's promises while also understanding their conditional nature.

Clarifying the Scope of Promises

It is crucial to clarify that not all of God's promises are conditional. Some, like the promise of the coming Messiah or the ultimate restoration of creation, rest solely on God's sovereign will. Yet, many promises that pertain to individual well-being, guidance, and blessing require a responsive posture from the believer.

Living with Unfulfilled Expectations

The reality of unfulfilled expectations, where suffering persists despite faithfulness, presents a significant challenge. This phenomenon is not an indication of God's unfaithfulness but a reflection of the complex interplay between divine sovereignty, human freedom, and the ongoing impact of sin in the world. It is also a reminder that the ultimate fulfillment of all promises finds its culmination in the eschatological hope of a new creation.

The Role of Scripture in Understanding Promises

The Bible, the inspired word of Jehovah, is the authoritative guide in understanding His promises. It is through a diligent study of the Scriptures, approached with the Historical-Grammatical method, that believers can rightly divide the word of truth (2 Timothy 2:15) and avoid the pitfalls of misapplying promises.

Conclusion

In conclusion, the interplay of conditional promises within the scope of divine foreknowledge and human free will forms a profound narrative. The believer's journey involves navigating this terrain, discerning the true nature of God's promises, and responding in faith and obedience. Such a path is marked by perseverance, a reliance on the Holy Scriptures, and an unwavering hope in the ultimate restoration that Jehovah has assured for those who love Him.

The Nature of God's Guarantees in an Imperfect World

In an imperfect world, where chaos seems to reign and suffering is an everyday occurrence, the nature of God's guarantees stands out as a beacon of hope for those navigating through life's tumultuous waters. The Bible, an ancient text with timeless relevance, offers insights into the assurances that God provides, not in the form of escapism from the world's imperfections but as a guide through them.

Understanding Foreknowledge and Freedom

Foreknowledge (*prognōsis*) in the scriptural context does not equate to predestination. It is vital to differentiate between God knowing what will happen and God determining what will happen. This is illustrated in the concept of simple foreknowledge, which suggests that *Jehovah* foresees events and circumstances yet does not orchestrate them. For instance, the Greek term *proginōskō* (to know beforehand) does not imply causation but rather, an awareness of future events. The Biblical God, therefore, is seen as an infallible forecaster of human history, understanding every possible outcome of human decisions without compelling these decisions. Like the shadow that precedes an individual around a corner, God's foreknowledge does not drive the person to turn the corner; the individual's choice leads to the shadow being cast.

Suffering and Human Independence

In the narrative of the Scriptures, the presence of suffering serves as a profound lesson rather than a condition engineered by God for growth. It highlights the brokenness that comes from human autonomy separated from divine sovereignty. The Hebrew term *ra* (evil or calamity) often encapsulates this concept of suffering, which is the byproduct of human actions rather than God's design. The object lesson humanity endures is akin to living in a world where the dissonance of human choices against God's perfect will leads to the cacophony of suffering.

Earthly and Heavenly Hopes

The Bible speaks of two destinies for redeemed humankind, which is not determined by a predestined plan but by God's response to human free will. There's the promise of a future where some will inhabit a heavenly realm (*ouranos*), while others will dwell on a perfected earth (*gē*). Texts such as Genesis 1:28 and Isaiah 45:18 underpin the idea that the earth was meant to be filled with people living under God's sovereignty. This destiny, however, remains open-ended, contingent upon individual and collective human choices, reflecting the Biblical theme of human agents working within the framework of divine foreknowledge.

God's Promises Amidst Human Tragedy

The daily horrors reported through media, from terrorism to natural disasters, pose the question of God's goodness in a world that is evidently imperfect. The Scripture provides a nuanced answer. God's guarantees do not promise an immediate cessation of all suffering but rather a future hope and present endurance. For instance, the Greek term *hupomonē* (endurance) denotes a quality that believers are to cultivate, not in a vacuum but in the very midst of tribulations. This endurance is not passive; it involves active dependence on God and a steadfast commitment to His principles amidst trials.

Imperfect World, Perfect Promises

Jehovah's promises are encapsulated in prophecies and assurances throughout the Biblical text. The visions of prophets like Isaiah and the promises made by Jesus in the Gospels (*euangelion*) speak of a future where God's sovereignty is fully realized and suffering is eradicated. However, these are not presented as immediate remedies but as assured ends that require faith and perseverance. The imperfect world is the stage upon which the drama of divine guarantees unfolds, with human actors free to choose their paths within the broad narrative crafted by God's foreknowledge.

In sum, the guarantees of God in an imperfect world are assurances not of a life without suffering but of a final destiny where suffering is no more. They are invitations to trust in the character and foreknowledge of Jehovah, who sees the end from the beginning, and yet allows for the moral agency of His creation. They do not represent a divine micro-management of human affairs but rather the ultimate triumph of God's will in a world that yearns for restoration amidst the disarray—a restoration in which both human freedom and divine sovereignty play integral parts.

Misinterpreting Divine Guarantees: Expectations vs. Scriptural Reality

In the journey of faith, the intersection of divine guarantees and human expectations is often fraught with misunderstanding. Believers may conflate promises of eternal provision with immediate, tangible relief in the temporal realm. Yet, Scriptural reality presents a more nuanced portrait of God's interaction with human suffering and imperfection. This chapter navigates through these complexities, aiming to reconcile the expectations we hold with the promises actually laid out in the Scriptures.

The crux of the matter lies in distinguishing what Jehovah has pledged from what believers sometimes presume He has pledged. For instance, while Scriptures affirm that "all things work together for good to those who love God" (Romans 8:28), this is not a blanket assurance that believers will evade hardship. Instead, it is a confirmation that, in the overarching schema of God's purpose, there will be a beneficial outcome for those who remain steadfast in faith.

Divine Promises and Human Misinterpretations

The term *prognōsis* (πρόγνωσις) in Greek, translated as "foreknowledge" in English, provides insight into the nature of God's promises. It suggests a prior knowledge, an anticipation of events, without implying causation. When examining the promises of God, it is essential to acknowledge the depth of divine *prognōsis*. God's promises are not simplistic cause-and-effect contracts but profound assurances woven into the fabric of His overarching plan, which accounts for the free will of His creation.

For example, when Jehovah told Jeremiah, "For I know the plans I have for you... plans for welfare and not for evil, to give you a future and a hope" (Jeremiah 29:11), He was not guaranteeing a life devoid of suffering. Rather, He was assuring Jeremiah of His benevolent oversight and ultimate purpose for His people, despite the immediate suffering they were enduring.

Perseverance Through Trial

James, the brother of Jesus, illuminates this concept further when he encourages believers to "count it all joy when you meet trials of various kinds" (James 1:2). The underlying Greek word for "trial" is *peirasmos* (πειρασμός), which conveys a testing or proving of one's faith. This Scripture doesn't imply God is the author of these trials but acknowledges that in a fallen world, trials are inevitable. The divine guarantee here is not the absence of trial but the presence of God and the maturation of faith through these experiences.

The Nature of God's Sovereignty

It is imperative to recognize that Jehovah's sovereignty is not compromised by human suffering. The sovereignty of God and human autonomy coexist in a manner that is complex yet harmonious. The historical-grammatical interpretation of Scriptures like "Jehovah has established his throne in the heavens, and his kingdom rules over all" (Psalm 103:19) affirms God's supreme authority without denying the real, lived experiences of suffering and evil.

The Role of Foreknowledge

In grappling with the concept of divine foreknowledge, it is beneficial to envision Jehovah as the perfect *barometer* of future events. This analogy encapsulates the nature of divine *prognōsis*—God's infallible awareness of future realities, which, like a shadow, does not force the outcome but rather indicates what will transpire due to the exercise of free will.

This perspective sheds light on the common misinterpretation of the role suffering plays in God's plan. Suffering is not a divine instrument preordained to shape character, but a consequential reality in a world where human independence from divine will has been exercised.

Understanding the Purpose of Earth and Humanity

In the original design, as articulated in Genesis, God created earth to be an abode for humanity, reflecting His glory and existing under His sovereign rule. Sin marred this perfection, but did not thwart Jehovah's purpose. The sacrifice of Jesus Christ provided the means for redeeming humanity, opening up the path to reconciliation with God and the restoration of all things. The Scriptures suggest that this redemption will culminate in a renewed creation, where suffering will no longer have a place.

The Reality of Suffering in a Fallen World

In the face of egregious evil and suffering, such as the atrocities committed by historical tyrants or the daily barrage of tragic news, many wonder where God is in all of this. It is a stark reminder of the imperfection that pervades our current condition—a condition marked not by divine guarantees of an easy path but by the promise of Jehovah's presence and the eventual righting of all wrongs.

Conclusion

Thus, when believers encounter the harsh realities of life, it is not an indication of God's absence or a failure of His promises. Instead, it is a reflection of the complex interplay between divine foreknowledge, human freedom, and the consequent reality of suffering in a world that eagerly awaits its final redemption. By holding closely to the literal and historical-grammatical interpretation of Scriptures, one can navigate through the trials with a hope anchored not in the absence of storm but in the assurance of the Shipmaster's return.

Perseverance Through Trials: The Biblical Perspective on Assurance

In the crucible of human experience, the mettle of faith is tested and the concept of perseverance becomes pivotal. The Biblical texts are replete with illustrations of perseverance, where individuals and communities are exhorted to steadfastness amidst tribulation, anchored in the assurances of God's character and promises. This steadfastness is a recurrent theme, found throughout the tapestry of Scripture, indicating that the endurance of faith is not just virtuous but vital.

The apostle Paul, who is accredited with penning 14 epistles including Hebrews, encapsulates this concept of endurance in the midst of trials through the Greek word *hypomonē* (ὑπομονή), denoting steadfastness, constancy, and endurance. In Romans 5:3-4, he explicates that "tribulation brings about perseverance; and perseverance, proven character; and proven character, hope." Here, the progression from suffering to hope is mediated by perseverance, a quality that is cultivated rather than conferred.

Perseverance, according to the Biblical narrative, is not a passive resignation but an active holding on to the promises of God despite the immediate circumstances. This perseverance is grounded in the nature of God, His *emet* (אֱמֶת)—faithfulness—and His *chesed* (חָסֶד)—lovingkindness—as depicted throughout the Old Testament, particularly in the Psalms. It is the certainty that the Creator, who called forth existence from void and fashioned the earth to be inhabited (Isaiah 45:18), has not abandoned His creation to futility.

In the Christian framework, Jesus Christ is portrayed as the quintessence of perseverance. The author of Hebrews presents Him as the "*archēgos* (ἀρχηγὸς) and *teleiōtēs* (τελειωτὴς) of faith," which can be rendered as the pioneer and perfecter of faith (Hebrews 12:2). His earthly sojourn, marked by suffering culminating in the crucifixion, and His subsequent resurrection, serve as a paradigm for believers. The exhortation to look to Him is an exhortation to see in His narrative the assurance that suffering is neither the end of the story nor devoid of purpose.

In grappling with the reality of suffering, the concept of *thlipsis* (θλῖψις)—tribulation—in the Biblical texts often conveys not just the presence of affliction but the pressure it exerts on the believer's faith. Yet, it is within this very pressure that the assurance of God's presence and eventual deliverance is accentuated. James, for instance, urges believers to consider it all joy when they encounter various trials, knowing that the testing of faith produces endurance (*hypomonē*). The book of Revelation, steeped in the language of trial and triumph, calls for the perseverance of the saints who keep the commandments of God and their faith in Jesus.

This perseverance is not in isolation but is often couched within a community of faith—a collective holding fast to the assurances of God. The early church, as depicted in the Acts of the Apostles, is a testament to a communal endurance amidst persecution and hardship. This communal aspect of perseverance is critical because it provides the support and encouragement that individual believers often need to continue in the face of adversity.

Furthermore, the Scriptures present God's foreknowledge not as a deterministic force but as an infallible awareness of all eventualities, a divine barometer that measures but does not manipulate the meteorological ebbs and flows of human volition. God's omniscience, His complete knowledge of all things, including future contingencies, stands outside of time, surveying the entire spectrum of temporal events and choices. This foreknowledge does not impinge upon human freedom; rather, it encompasses it.

The assurance for the believer, then, is not that suffering is absent but that it is understood and enveloped within the scope of divine providence. It is the assurance that the same God who foreknows also foresees the ultimate redemption and restoration of His creation. Just as Jesus, for the joy set before Him, endured the cross, scorning its shame (Hebrews 12:2), believers are called to look beyond the immediate horizon of their tribulation to the ultimate joy of redemption.

In conclusion, the Biblical perspective on assurance amidst trials is robust and dynamic. It does not trivialize suffering or offer platitudes. Instead, it recognizes the depth of human anguish but sets it within a larger narrative—a narrative where suffering is temporary, purposeful, and ultimately conquerable. It calls believers to a persevering faith, a faith that is refined in the fires of tribulation and anchored in the unshakeable promises of God. As such, to persevere through trials is not merely to endure but to triumph in the profound assurance of the faithfulness of God.

Bibliography

Anders, M., & Lawson, S. (2004). *Holman Old Testament Commentary - Psalms: 11.* Grand Rapids: B&H Publishing.

Andrews, E. D. (2016). *INTERPRETING THE BIBLE: Introduction to Biblical Hermeneutics.* Cambridge, OH: Christian Publishing House.

Andrews, E. D. (2017). *HUMAN IMPERFECTION: While We Were Sinners Christ Died For Us.* Cambridge, OH: Christian Ppublishing House.

Andrews, E. D. (2018). *LET GOD USE YOU TO SOLVE YOUR PROBLEMS: GOD Will Instruct You and Teach You In the Way You Should Go.* Cambridge, OH: Christian Publishing House.

Andrews, E. D. (2019). *SATAN: Know Your Enemy.* Cambridge, OH: Christian Publishing House.

Andrews, E. D. (2022). *THE LETTER OF JAMES: An Apologetic and Background Exposition of the Holy Scriptures (CPH New Testament Commentary).* Cambridge, Ohio: Christian Publishing House.

Andrews, E. D. (2023). *BIBLICAL APOCALYPTICS HANDBOOK: A Study of the Most Important Revelations that God and Christ Disclosed in the Bible.* Cambridge, OH: Christian Publishing House.

Andrews, E. D. (2023). *BIBLICAL EXEGESIS: Biblical Criticism on Trial.* Cambridge, OH: Christian Publishing House.

Andrews, E. D. (2023). *CHRISTIAN APOLOGETICS: Answering the Tough Questions: Evidence and Reason in Defense of the Faith.* Cambridge, Ohio: Christian Publishing House.

Andrews, E. D. (2023). *FAITHFUL MINDS: A Biblical and Cognitive Behavioral Therapy Approach to Mental Health and Wellness.* Cambridge, OH: Christian Publishing House.

Andrews, E. D. (2023). *LIFE DOES HAVE A PURPOSE: Discovering and Living Your Ultimate Purpose.* Cambridge, OH: Christian Publishing House.

Andrews, E. D. (2023). *MERE CHRISTIANITY REIMAGINED: Rediscovering the Faith for the 21st Century.* Cambridge, OH: Christian Publishing House.

Andrews, E. D. (2023). *THE BIBLE ON TRIAL: Examining the Evidence for Being Inspired, Inerrant, Authentic, and True.* Cambridge, Ohio: Christian Publishing House.

Andrews, E. D. (2023). *THE BOOK OF PROVERBS Chapters 1-15: CPH Old Testament Commentary: Volume 17.* Cambridge, OH: Christian Publishing House.

Andrews, E. D. (2023). *THE BOOK OF PROVERBS Chapters 16-23: CPH Old Testament*

Commentary: Volume 18. Cambridge, OH: Christian Publishing House.

Andrews, E. D. (2023). *THE EXPOSITORY DICTIONARY: A Companion Study Tool to the Updated American Standard Version.* Cambridge, OH: Christian Publishing House.

Andrews, E. D., & Marshall, T. F. (2023). *PAUL'S LETTER TO THE EPHESIANS: CPH New Testament Commentary.* Cambridge, OH: Christian Publishing House.

Andrews, E. D., & Torrey, R. A. (2016). *Christian Living: How to Succeed in the Christian Life.* Cambridge, OH: Christian Publishing House.

Arndt, W., Danker, F. W., & Bauer, W. (2000). *A Greek-English Lexicon of the New Testament and Other Early Christian Literature. 3rd ed.* . Chicago: University of Chicago Press.

Brand, C., Draper, C., & Archie, E. (2003). *Holman Illustrated Bible Dictionary: Revised, Updated and Expanded.* Nashville, TN: Holman.

Bratcher, R. G., & Hatton, H. (1993). *A Handbook on the Revelation to John.* New York: United Bible Societies.

Bromiley, G. W. (1986). *The International Standard Bible Encyclopedia (Vol. 1-4).* Grand Rapids, MI: William B. Eerdmans Publishing Co.

Bromiley, G. W., & Friedrich, G. (1964-). *Theological Dictionary of the New Testament, ed.*

Gerhard Kittel, vol. 4. Grand Rapids, MI: Eerdmans.

Campbell, A. (1850). *The Christian System (6th ed.;.* Cincinnati: Standard.

Easley, K. H. (1998). *Holman New Testament Commentary, vol. 12, Revelation.* (Nashville, TN: Broadman & Holman Publishers.

Erickson, M. J. (1992). *Introducing Christian Doctrine.* Grand Rapids: Baker Book Hous.

Harris, R. L., Archer, G. L., & Waltke, B. K. (1999, c1980). *Theological Wordbook of the Old Testament.* Chicago: Moody Press.

Kaiser, W. C., & Silva, M. (1994, 2007). *Introduction to Biblical Hermeneutics: The Search for Meaning.* Grand Rapids: Zondervan.

Kistemaker, S. J., & Hendriksen, W. (1953–2001). *Exposition of the First Epistle to the Corinthians, vol. 18, New Testament Commentary.* Grand Rapids, MI: Baker Book House.

Marshall, T. F., & Andrews, E. D. (2022). *PAUL'S LETTER TO THE PHILIPPIANS: An Apologetic and Background Exposition of the Holy Scriptures.* Cambridge, Ohio: Christian publishing House.

Mounce, W. D. (2006). *Mounce's Complete Expository Dictionary of Old & New Testament Words.* Grand Rapids, MI: Zondervan.

Ramm, B. (1999). *Protestant Biblical Interpretation: A Textbook of Hermeneutics*, 3rd rev. ed. Grand Rapids, MI: Baker.

Robertson, A. (1933, 1997). *Word Pictures in the New Testament.* Oak Harbor, MI: Logos Research Systems.

Stein, R. H. (1994). *A Basic Guide to Interpreting the Bible: Playing by the Rules.* Grand Rapids: Baker Books.

Sweeney, Z. T. (2005). *The Spirit and the Word (: , n.d.), 121–26.* Nashville: Gospel Advocate.

Terry, M. S. (1883). *Biblical Hermeneutics: A Treatise on the Interpretation of the Old and New Testaments.* Grand Rapids: Zondervan.

Thomas, R. L. (2002). *Evangelical Hermeneutics.* Grand Rapids: Kregel Publications.

Vine, W. E. (1996). *Vine's Expository Dictionary of Old and New Testament Words.* Nashville: Thomas Nelson.

Virkler, H. A., & Ayayo, K. G. (1981, 2007). *Hermeneutics: Principles and Processes of Biblical Interpretation.* Grand Rapids, MI: Baker Academic.

Whiston, W. (1987). *The Works of Josephus.* Peabody, MA: Hendrickson.

www.ingramcontent.com/pod-product-compliance
Lightning Source LLC
Chambersburg PA
CBHW051808040426
42446CB00007B/578